Art and Craft– The Business

LOTS OF PRACTICAL ADVICE TO HELP YOU BUILD AN EXCITING AND PROFITABLE BUSINESS

Elizabeth White

ISBN: 1871699061
ISBN 13: 9781871699067

dedication "For Emily"

Contents

Introduction

There has never been a better time to sell your creative work: people are appreciating the quality and originality of art and craftwork more than ever. Television has highlighted the importance of original design in our living spaces, and programmes about makers and designers have made people more comfortable with buying hand-made products.

Even in difficult financial times, many people are still prepared to pay that bit extra in order to purchase something unusual and different. Designers enjoy a higher profile than ever, and the Internet has made it possible for anyone to sell their work.

The creative factor

One of the dilemmas creative people face is whether to make what sells, or to try to sell what they make. People have succeeded with both routes – but it is no fun spending days painting cats if you don't like cats! Sometimes people new to selling are concerned when their wonderful work fails to find a market straight away; but it might be because they are trying to sell in the wrong place, rather than a problem with the work itself.

Starting out

Starting out selling your work is like taking a journey: unless you know where you're going, you are unlikely to get there. Setting targets and objectives is important. For instance, do you want to sell at craft fairs, have a website, or supply to shops? You might alter your targets as you go along, but it's important to know what you're aiming for.

Creative people often struggle with business planning, probably because most business plans start off from the wrong starting point. The simple business plan outline in Chapter 4 will help you on the road to success.

So assuming that you already have the necessary skills, and are competent to produce saleable goods, why not have a go at selling your work? If you have been trying to do so but have found it hard going, then use this book to improve your selling and marketing skills, and you will soon see the difference a professional approach can make.

Part 1

Making a living from your work

CHAPTER 1

Why run a creative business?

The cornerstone of an art or craft-based business is the ability to produce goods that are both saleable, and have a high level of quality and artistic design. Being a successful artist or craftworker involves making something suitable for the marketplace, and at the same time being comfortable with what you produce. Craftworkers and artists are creative people, and the chance to express their creativity is the main reason they choose to work in this field. But success in terms of selling your work depends on finding the balance between making what you like and making what will sell.

Why buy crafts?
Many people buy craftwork because they like something different: a unique piece of jewellery, or a vase that's not in every shop on the high street. Others like to collect the work of a particular maker. Some customers also enjoy actually meeting the person who makes the goods, and this can be a bonus for craftworkers who sell their products themselves either at their workshop or through craft fairs.

Why buy artwork?

People buy paintings and works of art for various reasons. They could be looking for something to give their room the "wow!" factor; or they could be collectors who follow a particular artist's career. Often someone will fall in love with a work of art and "have to" buy it – this is very satisfying for the artist. Other people will buy a painting simply because it matches the sofa – this often upsets artists, but if you are trying to make a living selling your work, you need to be realistic.

Competing with mass-produced goods

Working in an age of mass production has advantages and disadvantages. People have become used to cheap products; but at the same time many people are looking for something different, and this is the area in which the creative maker can succeed. In order to create a successful business, you will need to:

- Make something that appeals to a small group of people rather than trying to cater for a mass market.
- Always include as part of your work something that requires your specific skills, and is unique to you. You may eventually have help with the more mundane production areas, but there should always be an element that is yours and yours alone.
- Promote the fact that your products are unique, and that they have been created rather than produced.
- Seek out unusual materials, especially ones that cannot be used with mass production techniques.
- Research your market carefully and find out exactly where the gap is.

Finding the right niche can make all the difference between failure and success.

Finding your niche

If you haven't yet embarked on a particular craft, spend some time looking at craft fairs, attend some classes, and try as many different crafts as possible. You will probably be attracted to one more than others. Learn everything possible about your chosen craft, read all the books you can find, visit museums and galleries to see the products of famous artists and makers, and attend classes. Being a craftworker is a constant learning process, but once you actually start in the business the amount of time you will be able to devote to the learning process will be limited, so try to get a good start.

You may already be trained in a particular craft and know exactly what you want to do. However, if there is little demand for the type of work you make, you may need to reconsider. Some crafts will never be viable as a business, as the cost of the labour involved will make the goods unsaleable. Lace-making is one example of a craft for which it is difficult to obtain a realistic price: a garment may take 1000 hours to make and yet have a market value of £600. If this applies to your chosen craft, you may need to teach the craft in order to earn money, or use your skills in a different direction.

As an artist, you need to experiment with different mediums and styles; so attend as many exhibitions as you can and study the market carefully. Art, like other sectors, follows fashion; look at interiors magazines and see if your work is current. There will always be a demand for certain types of work such as local scenes and portraits, so if this is your forte then you should find a ready market.

Building a market from scratch is a time-consuming and expensive process, and without the resources of a large organisation it is virtually impossible to achieve. Finding a gap in the marketplace and filling it is certainly the more sensible option.

Creative satisfaction

When deciding which path to follow, remember that you will be doing this all day, every day in order to make a living, so you will need to ensure that even if you are working continuously at your craft or art you still receive creative satisfaction. In order to sell your work you may need to compromise on the type of work you make; but don't do this to the extent that your work becomes boring, or you will soon lose your enthusiasm.

Funding

Deciding which path to pursue will also be limited by the finance available. Set-up costs for crafts such as silversmithing are expensive, whilst silkscreen printing is relatively cheap.

You may be lucky enough to find funding from the Crafts Council, the Arts Council, or the Prince's Trust Enterprise Programme; or you may be in an area that offers local government start-up grants. Funding from these sources can usually only be used to help with start-up costs, not ongoing running costs. Alternatively you could follow the path of many craftworkers and artists, and work part-time to finance a period in which you start to create and sell.

Your customer

When planning your product, it is essential to have in mind a clear picture of the sort of person who will buy what you intend to make. An accurate customer profile will help you to:

- determine the design itself
- know the quantity you expect to sell
- know which type of fair, shop or gallery is the best outlet for your goods.

Constructing a profile of a typical customer can be a useful exercise. See "Market Research" in section 4 of this book for some ideas on how to do this.

The creative community

On becoming a creative, you will join one of the most exciting and interesting business communities there is. Creative people are generally very supportive; they help each other in a way that is unusual amongst competitors. Networking with others is important, particularly if you are working from home or by yourself. Attending shows and exhibitions will keep you in touch, or you could try joining a guild or artists' association. See Chapter 18, "Networking", for more ideas.

CHAPTER 2

Producing a saleable product

Who buys crafts or art?

Crafts and works of art are luxury purchases, and as such are in competition with many other goods and services. Your work will need to be innovative, attractive and of good quality to be successful in gaining its place in the marketplace. Individuals rather than organisations usually purchase this work, and people are more selective when spending their own money, which means that they will look for added value. Craft workers and artists have a natural advantage in this area, as their products are unique.

For most makers, the most exciting part of the process is actually creating the goods. However, making something that satisfies your creativity and then finding someone who likes it so much that they want to buy it, is guaranteed to give you a real buzz.

TOP TIP
If you are struggling trying to decide on a design or what to make, think of it as a gift for someone. It's amazing how easy the design will become if you have someone in mind to receive the product.

Finding out what sells

Before you start producing in quantity, it's a good idea to find out what will sell. See Chapter 20, "Market research", for some ideas on how to do this. Remember that sometimes, a very minor change to a product can increase its saleability and even the price you can charge for it: see Chapter 5, "Pricing for profit", for some ideas.

Developing a product range

Producing a range of products that relate to each other can increase sales by inspiring people to collect. Start by considering the designs that you are currently making, try to assess whether, and how, you need to modify them to make them saleable, and what new products you could design to form a range.

Most makers find that they need 'bread-and-butter" line to survive – something that is easy to produce and sells well in quantity. For example, a leather worker who makes briefcases may also make belts as a bread and butter line: or an artist may have their designs made up as greeting cards.

Time to design

As a maker, design will be a part of your work. You should try to build some time into your working week when you can experiment and focus on thinking about designing new products or ideas for paintings. Carry a notebook with you everywhere, and try out new ideas on friends, buyers and fellow makers.

In a creative business, product design is constantly evolving. Almost every day new ideas will occur, and you will always be testing out the possibilities of changing designs and improving your work.

To be successful, you need to be constantly improving and innovating. When designing a product you need to consider exactly what it is that makes the customer buy it. Do they need to buy a gift, or are they collecting craftwork and enjoying the image of having craft items around their house? By working out why your customers buy your products, and using this to influence your design, you should be able to increase sales.

You also need to consider the space people have in their homes. It's no use producing the most amazing piece of work if the customer cannot get it through their door! Buying a large piece also requires considerable confidence on the part of the customer; producing a collection of smaller pieces may encourage people to buy several.

Will your work sell?

- *Does it appeal to a small but accessible group of people?*
- *Does part of the process involve something that needs your exclusive talent?*
- *Is the skill, time and effort that go into your products reflected in the price?*
- *Do you use materials (for example, recycled materials) which are difficult for large manufacturers to use?*
- *Is there a market niche for your work?*
- *Is it instantly recognisable; does it have a very distinctive individual style, which collectors will recognise?*

If you can answer yes to all the above, you should have a good chance of success.

Unique selling point (USP)

A unique selling point (sometimes called "unique selling proposition") is what makes your product different from anyone else's. It adds value to your product, and adding value is the way to ensure that it is your product rather than your competitor's that succeeds. Because of the nature of craftwork, most creative businesses already have a unique selling point; but if you think that yours could be improved, try one of the ideas below:

- Produce a limited edition; give every piece a certificate.
- Add distinctive features. Think of Robert Thompson, the Yorkshire furniture maker who carved a mouse into every piece he made.

- If you're the first to produce something, include this fact in your marketing.
- Sign your pieces.
- Improve your point-of-sale material. Give written details of the product, its history, the materials used, etc.
- Find a historical link.
- Find a celebrity link (e.g. if a celebrity buys your work, ask them if you can use their name, or if they will Tweet about your work).
- Promote the regional or local significance of your materials or techniques.
- Give guarantees, warranties etc.

Evaluating a product

To work out whether a product is right for the marketplace, carry out some simple market research. When you make a new product, evaluate it yourself and also ask other people if they would buy it and how much they would pay. Try to ask people other than friends and relatives, who may be biased.

Make up a simple questionnaire asking people to give the product a score out of 5 on each of the following aspects:

- Appeal (how appealing do you find this product overall?)
- Appearance (how much do you like the way it looks?)
- Cost (how reasonable do you think the price is?)
- Design (how well-designed do you think it is? Does it work well, does it have any clever design features that you like?)
- Technique (how well-made do you think it is?)
- Uniqueness (how unique do you think it is?)
- Usefulness (how useful do you think it is?)

You yourself should also evaluate it on the following grounds:

- Availability of materials
- Hours of labour
- Profitability

The life cycle of a product

Few products go on selling forever without any updating or modifications. Sales will generally peak and then start to decline. The way to monitor this properly is to keep sales records, so that when a product declines you can cut back on production, or re-evaluate the product, rather than keep stockpiling something that is not selling. You will often hear a puzzled craft-worker saying, "But I've been selling it for years!" when sales start to drop off. Remember, tastes and fashion change; and this is true in crafts as well as other businesses.

If you conduct regular market research about your products, this will often reveal small changes you can make to them that will keep them updated and selling well. See Chapter 20 for some ideas on how to do this.

CHAPTER 3

Selling your ideas

I f you are good at designing but don't particularly want the hassle of producing a product, you can try to sell your designs. As a freelance artist you will submit your works to a company, and they will produce and market them to retailers. The advantage of this is that it allows you to focus on the creation and design of the product. The disadvantage is that they, not you, have control over the finished look and quality of the product.

The market for designs is huge, but to be successful you need to target your market carefully, making sure that you submit the right designs to the right company. Whatever your skill there is probably a market that is right for you. One card company, Simon Elvin, produce 2000 different designs each year using artwork, humour and verses, so they constantly need new talent. There is always a market for new ideas; why not give it a go? If you don't want to design cards, you could try a more unusual market such as designs for beach towels.

What type of work do they want?

A number of different kinds of companies buy designs. For example:

- Greeting card companies
- Textile business e.g. design for bedding

- Household goods e.g. ceramics
- Jewellery and fashion goods
- Publishers – illustrations for books

TOP TIP
Before sending any work to companies, always telephone or email to find out if they accept work from freelancers.

How to submit work
Research the market
First you need to identify the companies that use the work of freelancers and which would suit your style. It is no use wasting your time or theirs by submitting contemporary work to a traditional fabric company. To identify the right companies you can do a search on the Internet; most of the big companies have websites, which provide information not only on their ranges but also on how to submit work.

Many companies find designers at design shows like www.100percentdesign.co.uk, so try taking a stand at one of these shows. There is a list of all Greeting Card Association members looking for artists on www.greetingcardassociation.org.uk. Publications such as Progressive Greetings and Greetings Today also publish advertisements for card companies looking for ideas and artwork.

Prepare some designs
Before you start, produce a portfolio of designs so companies can see the style of work you produce. If the company likes your work they will either ask to buy one of your designs, or ask you to design to a brief.

Submit your work
Contact the companies that interest you, and ask them if they have guidelines for submitting work; sometimes these are published on their website. If writing rather than emailing, always enclose a SAE. Never send original artwork in an initial submission. Send several examples of your work to show

the breadth of your skills. Be guided by the information you receive from each company, but as a general rule, send 12 images.

Some publishers prefer to see finished designs; others prefer well- presented sketches. A publisher is usually looking for a distinctive style, creative thinking, knowledge of the market and a professional approach. It is a good idea to include at least one design in colour to aid visualisation for the publisher.

It is important to target more than one company at once. Rejection can be hard, so having more than one application on the go will help you keep positive. Don't forget to send different samples to each company; and while you are waiting, keep designing.

Your portfolio

If a company is interested in your work, they may ask you to visit them with your portfolio. This should comprise about twenty high-quality images of your most current work, either originals, or good-quality prints; plus a CD with this work on it. Include copies of your published work if applicable, and a CV or personal statement. All work should be current. Put you best work first, and show a consistent style.

Adjust your portfolio for each company, and show work that fits into their range. Present it professionally, and ensure you have some material to leave with them. Ask them what format they prefer: original work, CD, etc.

Feedback

Some companies will respond straight away; others on a monthly basis. Don't harass them, and don't get disheartened. They may contact you and ask for more specific submissions, but they will not pay you for this, as it is speculative.

Trade fairs

Some businesses are willing to meet artists at trade fairs and others are not. If you want to approach a particular company, make sure they are exhibiting at your chosen fair. Visit at the end of the week when it's quieter, and approach them on their stand. Have a few samples available, and ask them for a contact number and name. There is a list of trade fairs at the end of the book.

What is a range?

Before any artist puts pen to paper, the company establishes the structure of a prospective range. In order to balance each range, consideration is given to the overall theme. Usually one artist is assigned to each range, but a group of artists could work on a themed range.

Design brief

A design brief will then be drawn up and issued to the artists, who will then come up with some ideas. If these are suitable they will be expanded to more detailed designs before the artist embarks on the final piece of artwork.

How long should it take?

Artists work at different speeds, but it is unlikely that a design should take more than 2 days, although this may be spread over a period of ⬜me if the designs are sent back for alteration.

The money

A fee is negotiated separately for the worldwide reproduction rights of each design. This usually lasts from the date of publication until the design is discontinued. Figures given below are only an indication, you should always check before you start work to make sure there is a fee!

Payments and contracts depend on individual companies, but it is not unusual for a designer of a card, which sells millions at Christmas, to receive a design fee of between £200 and £250. Unless you are a well-known artist like David Hockney, when you can sell your designs under license, you will only receive a design fee.

There are no definite rules for payment: artists are paid in several different ways and can be paid per design or for a range. The most common methods of payment are:

- **Flat fee** – the publisher makes a one-off payment to the artist for ownership of a design for an unlimited period. This fee will normally be between £150 and £250 for a single design. The unit fee usually reduces if a range is to be produced.
- **Licensing fee** – this allows the publisher the right to use artwork for specified types of products and for a specific number of years, after which the rights revert to the artist. Artists are paid in the region of £150+ per design for this.
- **Licensing fee + royalty** – this is similar to the above, but with a royalty payment on each product sold. Artists would generally receive £100+ licensing fee plus 3% of the trade price of each card sold.
- **Advance royalty deal** – the artist is paid a goodwill advance on royalties. In the case of a range, the artist would receive a goodwill advance of say £500-£1,000 and would then receive an additional royalty payment of 5% once the threshold was reached.
- **Royalty only** – the artist will receive regular royalty payments based on the number of cards sold. Royalties are generally paid quarterly. Artists should expect a sales report and a royalty statement.

Dos and don'ts
Do:

- Do your research. Time spent examining the market will save you time and money in the long run.
- Always check if the company accepts work from freelancers, and check what format they require.
- Put your contact details on everything you send in, in case it gets separated.
- Always meet deadlines.
- Present everything properly.
- Enclose a large SAE with enough postage if you want your work returned, but realise that in a busy office it may get lost, so keep copies of everything.

Don't

- Don't ever send originals.
- Don't be long-winded: long letters rarely get read.
- Don't sell the same designs to two businesses.
- Don't take rejection personally. Ask for feedback: some companies give it, others don't.
- Don't be afraid to ask about payment.

Top Tip

Putting your details on websites such as www.peopleperhour.com can be a good way to find a regular supply of work

CHAPTER 4
Planning for success

The business plan

If you want to turn your creativity into a business, you will need a business plan. You wouldn't dream of starting out on an unfamiliar journey without a map or a satnav; and you shouldn't even consider starting to sell your work without a business plan. Creative people often think that a business plan will restrict them and stifle their creativity, but in fact, just the opposite is true; it is much easier to change direction and take advantage of opportunities if you know as much as possible about your business and its objectives. Even if you don't need to borrow money and are financing everything yourself, you still need a business plan, as you want to safeguard your own money.

Your plan can be formal, or it can just be a series of notes – it is your plan and you need to make it work for you. But either way, it needs to contain the following information:

The business – This section should include information on the type of business (sole trader, partnership, limited company?) and the background to the business premises (are you taking over an existing workshop, leasing a property, using your own home?) It should identify the goals you want to achieve, and give a brief general overview of your aims and objectives. Don't forget to say why there is a need for this type of business and why you will succeed.

The product – In this section you focus on the work you intend to produce. Specify the range of products you intend to market, the innovation and design element involved and how you intend to maximize this. Most importantly, you need to specify your Unique Selling Point, the thing that is going to guarantee your product a place in the market.

Marketing – This section will be concerned with how you plan to find your customers. A proper marketing strategy is important if you want your business to provide you with a living. You need to specify exactly who your customers are and then work out how you are going to reach them and persuade them to buy your goods. This section should also include details of your pricing structure, and include a strategy and budget for advertising and public relations. See Section 4 for more detailed information about these areas.

Operational details – This section should include details of your manufacturing facilities, equipment, and suppliers. All the aspects of the business have to blend together - the production levels need to match the number of sales, the finance needs to be there at the right time, and you need to have people available when needed, Having systems in place to track your production levels is essential for maintaining stock levels and knowing if you can fulfill an order. This can be done with simple charts showing how long it takes to make a batch of a certain item, what materials are needed to make it, and if the materials are in stock or have to be ordered.

Financial – In this section you should highlight all money matters. Include your capital requirements, details of the finance you have available, a forecast balance sheet for two years, and a proper cashflow. The cashflow is particularly important, as it helps you measure your results against the projected figures and use this to change priorities if necessary.

Management – Here, you should give details of any business training that you have undertaken to enable you to run a business, and the systems you intend to use. The main person in the business will obviously be you, and at this stage you probably do not intend to employ anyone else; but in this section of your plan you should detail what you intend to do when the business expands.

The future - Although you may find it difficult to think beyond the next twelve months, when you have a business you need to consider your long-term objectives. If you are starting off by selling at craft fairs, perhaps you intend to open your own studio one day; or your long-term plan may be to export to other countries. What sort of finance will you need long-term? A well thought out future plan can give a prospective funder confidence that you intend to work hard and make a go of it.

Short-term and long-term goals

It is important to have both short-term and long- term goals. Short-term goals are things that are achievable in the immediate future, and long-term goals are your ultimate destination. All your goals should be SMART, which means they should be:

Specific
Measurable
Achievable
Relevant
Timed

Short-term SMART goals could be:

- *To exhibit at a large craft fair next month*
- *To be selected for an exhibition in three months*
- *To set up a studio by the end of the month*
- *To be accepted by a website such as Not on the High Street this year*

Long-term SMART goals could be:

- *To have your own shop within 2 years*
- *To have your work on display in 10 shops by next year*

- *To be a designer for a high street retailer within 5 years*
- *To sell your work abroad using the Internet in the next 2 years.*

Presenting your plan

Unless you are trying to raise a considerable amount of finance, your plan will only need to be about 4 to 6 pages long. It should be supported by other documents such as your CV, details of your exhibitions and commissions, credit references, testimonials, etc. It should be presented in a professional manner; access to computers and instant print shops makes this easy and relatively cheap, and you must make every effort to see that your business plan reflects the professional image of your business. By all means use your creative skill to design an interesting cover, but let the facts and figures speak for themselves.

Uses for the plan

You will need to show your plan to prospective backers to help raise finance. Landlords may ask to see parts of a plan to establish your credibility. You may also need a business plan to join a craft centre or studio. Business advisers will find it easier to help you if they have a framework to work from. Your plan can also help you measure your progress, and give you confidence in your ability to succeed.

FAQs about business plans

1. Business plans are only for big businesses?

Wrong. Every business, however small, can benefit from having a business plan. The process of thinking through every aspect of the business is good discipline for the craftworker. You will be surprised how other ideas will develop and your goals will alter when you consider all the factors involved.

2. I'm too busy to write a business plan!

It will save time in the long run. Starting a business is time-consuming; life becomes hectic and there doesn't seem to be time to do everything. Without a proper plan, this state of affairs will continue ad infinitum. Writing a plan will help you to identify problems, correct errors, establish priorities and plan the best use of your time.

3. What if I want to change direction?

No problem. A business plan is not set in stone; it is a tool to work with. By putting down your thoughts on paper, you give yourself something to measure your progress against, and something to focus on when new opportunities arise. You won't be able to take advantage of all the opportunities that come along, so working out which ones will fit in best with your business plan will help you stay focused.

4. I don't know how to write a business plan!

It's easy. There is no right or wrong way to write a plan; the main person who needs to understand it is you. If you are writing a plan for the bank, or to obtain finance, ask them if they want it in a particular format. Your local Enterprise or Development Agency may be able to help; or ask your accountant. Don't rush; allow yourself enough time, and work on it in sections.

When you have written it, use it! Refer to it often, and keep updating it.

The "Tweet business plan"

If you don't want to write a traditional business plan, try writing one based on the principles of Twitter: each section should be no longer than a Tweet. Complete each of the following headings in 140 characters or less:

- *Your vision – Describe what you want to achieve. This makes you think about what you do and what's special about it.*
- *Is there a market? – If you're not sure, ask your customers/potential customers why they like your products.*
- *Your product – Describe your product and why it's so great. Think what you'd say if someone asked you, "What do you sell?"*
- *Target market – Be specific about who buys your products (gender, geography, age, etc.). Segment your markets if you plan on reaching them differently.*

- *Competition – Who would your customers buy from if your products didn't exist?*
- *Funding – List what you need, exactly what for, and when you'll be able to pay off the debt if you need to borrow.*
- *Sales channels – This is where you will sell your items – craft fairs, Internet, a local boutique, etc. It's good to have multiple channels. Include your longer-term sales goals; for example, perhaps you aim eventually to land several wholesale accounts.*
- *Marketing – How will you market your products – through a blog, on a website, via a brochure? You may need different actvities for different products.*
- *Pricing – How much does it cost you to make and market your products? How much do you plan to sell in a given time period? How do you plan to price them?*
- *Targets – Set targets and deadlines, to help you stay on track.*
- *People – Who do you know that you could call on for help, and what kinds of help could they give?*

CHAPTER 5

Pricing for profit

One of the biggest problems people face when starting to sell their work is how to price it. It is a difficult question to answer, as it can be hard to work out the real cost of making creative work. But unless you are covering your costs, every time you sell a product you are literally giving money away. Basing your prices on what another maker is charging, without calculating your own costs, is the sure way to disaster.

Pricing craftwork

The joke about the craftworker who won the lottery and, when asked what they would do, replied, "Keep doing the craft fairs until the money runs out," unfortunately has a ring of truth about it! The people who are prepared to work for little or no return do no favours to themselves or to other makers. Even if you are only using your hobby to provide extra income, you should still be charging a reasonable price.

To calculate the prices you should charge, you need to calculate your costs. These fall into three categories:

- Production costs
- Overheads
- Selling costs

Then you should add a profit margin on top.

Production costs

These are the easiest costs to calculate. It will probably be easier to calculate the costs for a batch of products rather than trying to work out an individual cost, unless you work to commission, in which case each piece of work will have to be calculated separately. Production costs cover two main areas: the materials used, and the labour costs.

Materials – to calculate the cost of materials, simply charge to each object the cost of the raw materials required to make it. Depending on your craft you may also need to allow for wastage. You need to base this on knowing exactly what you're spending, so get a notebook and write down everything you buy. A separate purse or wallet and a separate bank account will stop you from purchasing materials and not including them in the cost.

Labour – the easiest way to calculate an hourly labour cost is to decide how much you would hope to earn in the year, divide this by the number of weeks per year you intend to work, and then by the number of hours per week, to give an hourly rate. When deciding how much you need to earn, be sure to include all your needs: rent or mortgage, council tax, food, bills, etc. Then assess how many hours it takes you to make each item, multiply this by your hourly labour cost, and add this to the production cost of the item.

Overheads

These include all the costs involved in running your business and workshop, which have to be paid whether you are working or not. Calculating the overheads becomes easier after you have been in business for a year or more, as you can base your calculations on last year's figures; but it needs to be done from the beginning, so have a go.

Overheads can be divided into four headings: workshop expenses, business expenses, equipment and stock.

Workshop expenses – these include rent or mortgage, council tax, utilities (gas, electricity, water), maintenance and repairs. If you are working from home then you should estimate a percentage of your household bills and use that figure. For instance if you have 6 rooms in the house and you use one of them your percentage could be 16%

Business expenses – these include telephone, Internet, postage, travel and car costs, insurance, and professional fees such as accountants.

Equipment/loans – if you have borrowed money to start a business, you need to include the repayment costs in your overheads. If you use expensive equipment, which may have to be replaced or added to, allow a percentage of the replacement cost. This should then be 'saved' so you can afford to replace the equipment when it becomes necessary. For example, if you have a kiln costing £500 and you need to replace it every 5 years, it 'costs' you £100 a year.

Stock – stocks of raw materials or products, which are just sitting on a shelf, are costing you money. Calculate 20% of your average stock value and add this to the overheads.

When you have calculated your annual overheads, divide the figure by the number of weeks per year that you work, and then by the numbers of hours per week. This will give you an hourly overhead rate, which you should add to the cost of each item.

Selling costs

These should include craft fair/market stall fees and travel costs, photography, production of publicity material, agent's fees or commission, shelf rental, website hosting costs, etc. If you need to stay overnight when you go to fairs, these costs should be included either here, or as business expenses. Many makers find it difficult, particularly in the early stages, to work out their selling costs: if this is your problem, just add a fixed percentage, say, 20%, of the production and overhead costs, as shown in the example at the end of this chapter.

Profit margin

When you have calculated all the costs involved in producing your work, you need to add a profit margin of around 20% to cover breakages, unexpected bills, etc. Profit is very important: it provides the cushion against anything that goes wrong, from needing a new kiln to breaking your arm and being unable to work.

Using the cost price to calculate the selling price

Once you have calculated your cost price and added your profit margin, you can then decide the selling price. This will be influenced by where you sell the products and what your competitors charge. The actual mark- up may vary from piece to piece; some of your lines may be prove to be more profitable than others and obviously these are the ones you wish to concentrate on. If you sell both to shops and at craft fairs, you may have to either produce different ranges for each market, or increase your craft fair prices in line with the shop price.

VAT

If your turnover is above £81,000 a year (2015), you need to be registered for VAT, and you must add VAT to all sales. At present VAT is 20%. For more information, see www.hmrc/vat.co.uk

Pricing example

This costing method is designed for makers who are working full-time. If you share premises or work part-time, you will need to adjust the figures. The labour cost will depend on how much you want to earn per hour. BE REALISTIC!

A maker produces 20 jugs a day. To calculate the individual cost of each jug, first calculate the cost of the batch.

Production costs

Materials	£20
Labour 8 hrs. @ £8 p/h	£64

Overheads

Hourly rate £1/hr.	
(Weekly rate £40)	£8

Sub-Total	**£92**	
Selling Costs	**20%**	**£18.40**
Total cost for 20 jugs	**£110.40**	
Cost per jug	**£5.52**	
Profit margin	**20%**	**£1.10**
Total per Jug	**£6.62**	

So the selling price of the jug needs to be at least £6.62

A reality check

You now know that your jug needs to sell for at least £6.62. However, you also know that a gallery or shop will add 50-100% to the price, and maybe VAT too; so a more realistic selling price is £15. Will the jug sell at this price? It might sell for even more, if you have a name; but if it will only sell for £10, this leaves you with a problem. You should never sell a product you are losing money on, but there may be small changes you could make that would make the product viable. So before you decide to ditch the product, try some of the following:

- Could you make it more cheaply, perhaps by using a different glaze?
- Can you speed up the process so you can make more in the time?
- Can you find cheaper suppliers of the materials?

If you cannot cut costs, then maybe you can add value:

- Improve the packaging
- Use a more expensive glaze which could command a higher price
- Add something extra – a candle to a burner, a purse to a handbag

Remember when costing your work:

- You will not sell every item that you make.
- If the process you use has quality problems, you will need to allow for this.
- If you plan to sell through both shops and craft fairs, you need to ensure that the selling price at both is comparable.
- If your turnover exceeds £81,000 per year (2015), you need to be registered for, and add VAT.

Pricing artwork

Pricing artwork is even more difficult, because although you can calculate it in the same way as a craft product, this is rarely realistic. You also need to take account of:

Reputation/track record – an artist just leaving college is unlikely to command as high a price as an artist with an international reputation. So compare your prices to the work of similar artists.

The market – the art market is unpredictable. The same painting could command a different value in different parts of the country or different galleries. Carrying out as much research as possible into the prices charged in galleries and on websites will help you find your place in the market.

Rarity – one-of-a-kind pieces are worth more than multiples, such as prints, by the same artist.

Cost of materials – the addition of expensive materials, such as gold leaf, may add to the value of a painting.

Framing – an expensive frame can add value to a work. Framing is something a good gallery can advise you on. If they offer a framing service, they may prefer your work unframed.

Productivity – if your work is labour-intensive and you only produce a few paintings a year, you should be able to charge more for them than someone who produces in volume.

Permanence – paintings on canvas usually fetch higher prices than those on paper, as people think they will last longer. For the same reason, people are reluctant to invest in textile artwork.

Size – when pricing contemporary work, bigger is almost always more expensive, although smaller works may sell well. Very large works may appeal to the corporate market; this may mean an artist can charge more for the work, as the buyers will have larger budgets.

Always set your prices before showing to a gallery. You will know from their reaction whether you work is saleable at that price. It is not the gallery's job to set your prices, but once you have a relationship with them, they will probably offer advice. Listen!

TOP TIP
Remember, you can always raise your prices but you can never lower them, because that lowers the value of the work your collectors have already bought and destroys market value.

Commissions

A commission could be anything from a portrait to a book cover. If the commission comes through a gallery, they will have an input as to price. If it comes directly to you, remember that the customer wants your work, and you should value it accordingly.

Costing for commissions is basically the same process as pricing any other work you produce, except that you will be costing in advance and estimating the time and materials. This obviously becomes easier with experience, but be careful: it's easy to make expensive mistakes.

Overestimate rather than undercharge, and don't forget to allow for design and research time. If you break even on your first commission, you should be pleased; it is so difficult to work out the costs, that makers often end up working for as little as £1.50/hour. When you become more experienced, you can produce a sliding scale, which will make it much easier to calculate your fees.

TOP TIP
Even if you lose money on your first commission, keep records and use it as a learning experience. Next time, your costs will be more accurate.

CHAPTER 6
Presentation and display

Why display counts

f you have spent time and effort creating beautiful handmade items for sale, allow enough time to plan your display and do justice to your hard work.

Artwork and creative products are very visual, and displaying them properly is vital. Whether in your studio, at a craft fair or in an exhibition, every opportunity must be taken to present your products in the best light to maximize the potential sales. This doesn't mean you have to spend a lot of money on expensive equipment; it is amazing what can be done with a little ingenuity. The exception to this is when exhibiting at a trade fair: professional presentation is very important, and if you are not able to design and build a stand of suitable quality then you will need help.

Craft fairs

When exhibiting alongside other craftworkers, a professional display will attract people to your stand and improve business. Before you go, try to find out what space you will have, and particularly if there is any wall space. At some craft fairs you will be limited to a table space, and you will only be able to stand behind it to sell. If this is the case, the table should be completely covered to hide any boxes or packing underneath. If you intend to exhibit regularly at craft fairs, design a portable stand, which is flexible, as you might not always have the same size space.

Trade fairs

At a trade fair you will simply be supplied with a shell and power points as ordered. You then have the opportunity to create either a walk-in area if the space is big enough, or a professionally designed stand. Consider how you can display your work to the best advantage, and don't forget to consider security. Retailers like to see how the goods could be displayed in their shop, so think about this when you plan your displays. If you produce special display stands for your products then your trade customers might be interested in purchasing/borrowing them with the crafts. You could offer a package deal.

Art exhibitions

Displaying artwork at exhibitions can be difficult. It is always important to try to get wall space so you can hang work; failing this, you will have to create some display boards yourself. Artwork will not sell flat on a table. A browser is a good idea so people can browse through your unframed work. If you sell cards, buy a small stand to display them properly.

General rules for creating a great display:

Height – You want people's eyes to roam all around the space you have, so don't lay your items flat – use furniture, boxes and shelving to create variations in height.

Branding/image – Think about who your target audience is, and focus on attracting attention from them. If your items are expensive, they will probably suit a more sophisticated display. You should consider the overall impression you are giving to potential customers.

Themes – The theme should complement your items, not outshine them. Picking a theme will help to focus your ideas and simplify your display. Ensure that your display is still approachable and not too intimidating for customers to interact with you or your items. "Do not touch" signs are a definite no, but if you do have breakables then put them towards the back or under glass.

Colour – Try to colour-coordinate everything you use. If your products are very colourful, go for a neutral shade like cream or black; but sometimes a bright background lifts the products, so experiment with different fabrics.

Props – Use props to display your items: for instance, placing an old mobile phone into one of your phone cases will help customers instantly identify the function. Don't overdo the props; allow the products to speak for themselves.

Price labels – Customers may not want to ask how much an item costs for fear they cannot afford it; so label items clearly, and display a price list if possible. Take time and effort to match your labels with your display. Beautiful labels will add to your overall presentation; shabby labels will detract from it. The most important factor is legibility, so if you have terrible handwriting, print out your labels. Ensure your spelling and grammar are correct!

Signage/Banner – You want people to remember your stall, but also your company name. It's important to display a banner or sign on your display. Reasonably priced pop-up banners can be purchased online and used even in small spaces.

Space – Use all your available space, or "Think outside the table". Can you add a stand to the side or in front of the table? This is especially useful for selling cards or accessories. Can you remove the table so people can walk around your stands/racks? Of course, be careful not to encroach on your neighbour's stalls!

Lighting – A well-lit display will really help to show off your items. Enquire about power points in advance. Your lights should illuminate your work, or highlight your best pieces – ensure that they are not blinding for customers. Chain-store spotlights can often be used to keep costs down; or visit factory lighting shops.

Access – Can people reach your items? Do you want them to? Think of ways to maximise the number of people that can be at your stall or table. Picking an item up or being able to get really close to it can only help with a sale – but beware of children's sticky fingers. Place your valuable items in elevated and stable positions.

Safety – Keep wires out of the way and ensure your table covering is not too long causing a trip hazard. Attach the cloth to the table to avoid small hands pulling it and your goods off.

Improvised display material

Start by considering your own goods: can any of them be used for display? Look around your home: mug trees can be used for jewellery, clothes- horses for scarves or clothes. Visit the garden centre and see what they have on offer: a trellis can be used in many ways, especially if you paint it to match your business colours. Cover sturdy boxes with fabric or paper in your colours. Use plant pots and shelves to build a display. The possibilities are endless, and a little imagination can easily produce whatever best suits your needs. But if you sell cards, don't try to improvise with these, as good display is essential. A spinner will almost always increase sales. Secondhand spinners are often advertised on eBay under "shop fittings", or you could try asking at local card shops.

Commercial display products

When you begin in crafts, spending money on display items may seem to be extravagant. In fact, it is vital. A professional display can give added value to your goods. Craft and Design magazine carries advertisements for suppliers of displays and packaging, which are tailored to craftworkers' needs. Alternatively, most large towns have a shop-fittings store that may stock stands that you can use.

Custom-built display stands

If you can afford it, consider having a specially designed stand. These can be made so that they fold away easily, and are a boon if you are exhibiting every weekend. You may be able to design something yourself and find a local joiner who will build to your design. Remember it will need to fit in your car or van, and if you exhibit alone then you will need to be able to transport it easily. Look around at your competitors and see what works for them, and decide if it will work for you. Good ideas can always be adapted.

Point-of-sale material

A good display will always contain some point-of-sale material. Photographs of your studio and products can enhance a display and draw customers to your stand. A flier with details of your background, training and motivation along with details of where your work is available is useful. Don't forget a price list/order form with a sketch of the product to remind people about your work. Shops and galleries may require photographs and more upmarket material.

Packaging

Some items, such as jewellery, benefit from being packaged; but this will add to the cost, so make sure you add the cost into the sale price. A search online will provide a wide range of boxes and bags, many of which can be printed with your logo. If you are planning to build a brand, make sure any packaging fits in to the overall image of your business.

A large roll of bubble-wrap will be useful for packaging artwork and ceramics. Buy this in bulk to save money.

Top Tip

Always have a practice before your first fair or show, and make sure that any stands or furniture fits the allotted space.

Part 2

The Basics

CHAPTER 7

Starting out

When starting to sell, you are effectively creating a business even if you are operating part-time from home you need to be aware of what running a business entails. There are several different legal structures that a business can have, and the one you choose will affect how much tax you pay, how much paperwork your business is required to do, the personal liability you face, and your ability to raise funding.

Types of business structure

A sole trader is the most common form of business organisation. It's the simplest to set up, and offers complete managerial control to the owner. However, the owner is also personally liable for all financial obligations of the business. As a sole trader you simply register with HMRC www.hmrc.gov.uk within 12 weeks of starting up, and then fill in an annual tax return to calculate the amount of tax you need to pay. If you only earn a small amount, you can claim an exemption.

A partnership involves two or more people who agree to share in the profits or losses of a business. If you set up a partnership, it is important to draw up a partnership agreement. This can be as simple as a letter signed by both of you, or you can download an official agreement from websites such as www.lawdepot.co.uk or www.freelegalforms.net. The main things to include are who does what, how the money will be divided, and how decisions are taken. Perhaps the most important thing is how you will end the partnership – will one person buy the other out, or just remove their name? Who will have the customer list? These are all issues, which can be very difficult to resolve. If you are investing a lot of money, you should get legal advice and have a solicitor draw up the partnership agreement.

A limited liability company (LLC) is popular because it allows owners to take advantage of the benefits of both the corporation and partnership forms of business. The advantage of this business format is that profits and losses can be passed through to owners without taxation of the business itself, while owners are shielded from personal liability. However the disadvantage is that you will have to file your accounts with Companies House, and unless you can do this yourself you will need to employ an accountant. You can find details of how to set up a limited liability company at www.hmrc.gov.uk/factsheet/limited-company.pdf

A social enterprise is a business that trades for a social and/or environmental purpose. It will have a clear sense of its 'social mission', which means it will know what difference it is trying to make, who it aims to help, and how it plans to do so. It will also have clear rules about what it does with its profits, reinvesting these to further its 'social mission'. If you meet these criteria, and have these commitments expressed clearly in your governing documents, then you are very probably a social enterprise. For craftworkers, a group studio could be a social enterprise; or if you want to teach art to children, you could start a social enterprise.

A co-operative is a type of business structure, which is often overlooked. It can prove to be appropriate for craftworkers or studio groups, either for working or for retailing. The umbrella organisation, which offers help and advice to prospective co-operatives, is the Industrial Common Ownership Movement (ICOM). Forming a co-operative is a popular option for artists and craftworkers.

How to set up a co-op

Co-operatives usually start when a group of like-minded people meets to explore the possibility of working together. It may be because they have a common need such as childcare or a common problem such as redundancy. If you don't know enough people who are interested then you could try advertising. The local paper may publish an appeal for members, particularly if the subject is interesting.

There are no special qualifications necessary to become a co-op member. Personality and commitment are more important than skills. It is important to discuss the co-op's shared aims thoroughly; do not assume that you know what the other members believe, even if they are old friends! That said, a co-op could give you great flexibility and more control over your working life, while still allowing you to share skills and responsibilities with others.

Principles of a co-op

A workers' co-operative is a business, which is owned and controlled by the workforce.

Regular meetings are held, at which all members can vote.

The finance needed to operate the co-op is borrowed on simple loan terms.

When a co-op ceases trading and is dissolved, members cannot benefit financially. Any money remaining must be transferred to another co-op or to a central fund.

A workers' co-operative has social as well as financial obligations.

Profits made by a co-op are retained in the business, distributed between the members, or used to support the social objectives of the co-op.

CHAPTER 8

A place to work

Finding a suitable location

Have you ever wondered why makers seem to thrive in some parts of the country and not in others? In some businesses, such as retailing, it is obvious that you need to be situated in a popular shopping area with plenty of passing trade; but with other businesses the importance of location is not always apparent, yet being in the right place can be crucial to success. Internet-based businesses can in theory be based anywhere, but you still need to consider convenience. Driving an hour a day to deliver packages to a depot is not cost-effective. So make sure the area you chose is well served by distribution companies.

Which area?

The problem of where to locate your business is just as important to creative businesses as it is to other organisations, particularly if you intend to sell direct to the public. The area must have the right type of customer. It is no use setting up a high-class gallery in an area of high unemployment.

A complete change?

People who want a complete change of lifestyle often decide to relocate in order to start a business. Many people dream of living and working in the country, or moving to their favorite holiday town. If you are planning to move and start a business, investigate the area carefully. A town that is busy in summer may be dead for six months of the year.

Making the decision

If you are already running a business, moving premises may be the first big step you take. It is easy to fall into the trap of many small business owners by considering the size, type, suitability and running costs of the premises before their location. The right way is to look at the location first, and then to consider the property available.

What do you need?

You can find the right location by deciding what is important to your business. Consider the following factors:

- Access to markets: how close do you need to be to your customers? Are the right type of people living in the area?
- If you plan to supply the high street, ease of distribution may be important.
- If you send a lot of work out to Internet customers, living 20 miles from the nearest post office or collection centre might not be a good idea.
- Availability of grants and subsidies: some areas award a wide range of grants to businesses moving into the area, so if this could affect you, check with your local business development agency.
- Convenient to suppliers: if you rely on frequent deliveries from a supplier, would it make sense to locate close to them?
- Cost: rent and rates may vary considerably from place to place.

- Transport: do you need to be close to the motorway network or a railway station?
- Environment: is a town or the country more appropriate for you?

When you find a location, use this checklist to compare locations:

- Nearness to customers
- Number of competitors in the area
- Rent and rates
- Convenience for transport
- Ease of access
- Attractiveness of the area
- Availability of parking
- Cost and availability of insurance
- Availability of staff
- Security

The "feel-right" factor

As any business owner will tell you, it is also important to consider the 'feel-right' factor. Many successful businesses have been started in unlikely places because it 'felt right'. This doesn't mean that you must ignore everything else; carrying out an investigation as listed above will give you the knowledge necessary to make an informed decision, and hopefully it will also 'feel right'! Some areas have flourishing artistic communities, and this will increase the competition but also the level of support.

Type of premises

Choosing a workspace will depend on a number of factors, mainly what is available in your chosen location, what you can afford and facilities required.

Working from home

This is still a popular option for makers who are starting out. If you are fortunate to have an outbuilding or spare room, this could be a viable option.

In most cases you do not need planning permission to set up a business from home particularly if you are operating at a fairly low level of production and not causing a nuisance. However there are exceptions for instance if you were setting up as a metal worker with a forge in the garage you might be contravening a byelaw. it is always advisable to operate legally so check with the relevant authorities if you have any doubts. Remember that failure to give information on business stock kept at home may also mean that your home contents policy is invalid. You could also be in breach of your tenancy or mortgage agreement so check with your building society or landlord.

Renting a workshop

If you cannot work from home, renting a workshop will be your next option. Decide whether you want to work alone or in a group setting, and look at what is available. When starting up it is always advisable to try to find somewhere with a short lease or easy in-and-out terms. Networking is a good way of finding out if people have space available.

Individual studios

You may be able to find an individual studio suitable for your needs at a reasonable rent. Security may be a problem here, particularly if it is relatively isolated, so if you can find one in close proximity to other makers then so much the better. If you intend to retail from your premises, make sure they have planning permission or that you are likely to obtain the necessary permission for retailing.

Group workshops/craft centres

In the last few years there has been a substantial growth in studio provision at craft centres. The visual arts officer at the Arts Council or a local arts association should have a list of premises in your area. Some of these are open to the public all the time; others only open for exhibitions. If they are open all the time, make sure you will have sufficient time to produce the goods as well as serving the public; there should always be one day when you are not expected to open. Some have joint display space staffed by someone else, which can be useful, allowing you to get on with your work.

When looking for a craft and design centre, check the following:

- Opening times
- Opportunities for joint publicity
- Who runs it: paid staff, or a committee of makers?
- Will you be expected to take on a share in the running, and if so, what is the time commitment?
- Exhibitions
- Other facilities e.g. photocopiers, computers, etc.
- Location
- Length of tenancy: can you exit quickly?
- Other tenants: is there a mix, or is it biased towards one craft?
- Do the current customers fit with your customer profile?

Helping customers find you

If you're selling from your studio, you need to ensure that people can find their way to the business. Always provide a good location map, with details of car-parking, prior to a customer's visit, and also make it available on your website. Ensure that your studio is well signposted. Planning authorities should be consulted before erecting signs on the public highway or in conservation areas. Other regulations concerning illuminated signs etc. vary from area to area.

Also, get your business marked on Google maps. Sign in to your Google account, go to Google Maps, and follow the "Put your business on Google Maps" link on the left. Google will send you a postcard to verify you really are there, and when you send it back, and they add you to the map.

TOP TIP

Don't rely on others to promote the centre. You still need to promote your business and attract customers to your studio.

CHAPTER 9

Keeping control

very business requires some basic paperwork. Your accounts need to be up to date, your cashflow calculated, and details of your customers and orders available. It may seem a waste of time when you're starting a business and trying to do twenty things at once, but keeping everything in order and easily accessible will actually save you time.

Systems

Put your systems in place before you start your business, and set aside a regular time each week to bring everything up to date, and you will make life easier for yourself and run your business more efficiently.

Office equipment

You don't need a special room in which to do your paperwork, but you do need some space in your studio or home where you can keep everything together. Cut-price printers and second-hand office suppliers can supply everything you need at a reasonable cost. Pound shops can be a good source of cheap stationery.

It is almost impossible to run a business without a computer, or at least access to one. Design software can save you money by allowing you to create your own leaflets and other printed materials, and accounts software can help you organise your finances: so think about what you really need and then find the cheapest way of obtaining it.

A good printer is essential too – look out for a deal on the high street, but remember it is the inks rather than the machine, which will cost the money. A laser printer works out cheaper in the long run, although it may not give the same results creatively as an inkjet. Buy a printer, which incorporates a scanner, for multi-purpose use.

Basic equipment:

- a desk/table
- a chair
- a filing cabinet - this will make life so much easier, so find a second-hand one if you can't buy new
- a landline telephone with an answering machine, so you don't miss orders (A landline gives credibility to your business in many customers' eyes, because it is traceable)
- a dedicated mobile that is just for your business, with facilities to accept credit card payments
- access to a computer, and a reliable Internet connection
- lever-arch files, or enough space on your computer, or on the cloud, to file all your records
- files and boxes
- invoice/order books for use at craft fairs, and suitable templates on your computer for other orders
- paper
- stapler, paperclips, hole-punch, pens etc.
- IN and OUT trays

When you purchase these, don't worry about image; go for value. No one will see them and they don't make any money.

Stationery

You will need:

- **Letterheads:** if most of your communication is digital, have a nicely-designed letterhead in Word or PDF that is not too big a file, so that it can be emailed easily. If you mainly use hard copy, you can print your letterhead off as needed – or you can get a large number of them printed professionally, and put them into your printer instead of plain paper.
- **Business cards:** there are a number of websites, which offer free business cards or charge only postage. These are fine to start you off, but do use your own design and pay to have their logo removed from the back if you want to look more professional. Paying extra for better quality card is always worth it.
- **Compliment slips**: surprisingly useful, and they save letterheads.
- **Envelopes**: buy the cheapest available, in a variety of sizes.
- **Cash box:** many people create difficulties for themselves by handling business money with personal cash. They don't keep proper records, and when they have to produce annual accounts or fill in their self- assessment forms they run into trouble, which can end up costing them a lot of money. Keep a cash box for business money if you don't need a till, and jot down every time you take money out or put it in. Keep every single receipt: they can be claimed against tax.

Many printers offer an inclusive deal to new businesses, so shop around. For design ideas, see Chapter 21 on creating an image for your business.

Files

Your filing system can be digital, or on paper (hard copy) – but it is best to stick to either one or the other. So if you use hard copy and someone emails you an invoice, you need to print it out; and if your system is digital and someone posts you something, you should scan it and/or add the information to your accounting program.

File things away as they come in, in month order, so it's easy to see what you owe and what is owed to you.

You need:

- Four files:
    1. Invoices you receive - transfer to
    2. Invoices received and paid
    3. Invoices you send out - transfer to
    4. Invoices sent out and payment received
- A separate file for bank statements, unless you use online banking exclusively
- A file for orders, filed either monthly, or under each customer's name. Transfer to another file when completed. Don't throw them away: someone might want to repeat their order. If you work digitally, this could be supplanted by a customer database or CRM software.

At the start of your financial year, start new files.

Bookkeeping system

The simplest system consists of an account book (Simplex D, Everite or something similar). Alternatively, if you keep your financial records digitally, use a free accounting package such as QuickBooks or VT Cashbook, or simply use Excel spreadsheets. If you are using an accountant, ask them to suggest a system; then you can simply email your accounts across to them, which will save you time and money.

Time management

Many people enter self-employment because of the simple desire to be free from the nine-to-five routine. Creating and selling your own work can soon take over your life, and it is important to create some balance in order to retain your sanity and the support of your family. Here are some ideas to help you organise your time:

- **Prioritise tasks.** Traditional wisdom suggests that you should do the most important tasks first, and get them out of the way. In many cases this is a good idea; but scheduling tasks when you are at your best is important too. So if you are at your most creative in the morning, do your creative work then, and leave the paperwork and packaging until the evening. This is fine until you have a large order to get out, and find yourself producing for 12 hours a day! This is inevitable when you are first starting up, but eventually you should learn how to control your production and not promise more than you can deliver.

- **Create a routine.** Routines don't have to be boring, and they can be incredibly useful at ensuring you get your work done. By setting a routine you can at least hope to introduce some "work-life balance" into your life; and a regular start time can help to get you in the mood for work and keep things on target. You can create a routine that you can slot in around your other commitments; a standard nine-to-five may work for some people, while different hours may work for others. Find what suits you and stick to it. But don't be afraid to break your own rules from time to time; breaking rules is fun and can end up being productive.

- **Time diary.** If you are really struggling with time management, keep a time diary for a week. Write down literally everything you do, and divide it into sections at the end of the week to see how much time you have spent on each area of your work. Creating, marketing, admin, research, and thinking time should all be in proportion. If you are creating for 4 hours a week and thinking for 20, you might find it difficult to make any money.

TOP TIP

If you really struggle with the admin and bookkeeping then consider employing someone half a day a week as soon as you can afford it.

CHAPTER 10

Money Matters

Even if finance is not your strong point, you really need to know how it all works if you are to succeed. Control of finances is the key factor in the success or failure of any business; and although it may seem daunting, it is easily done if you learn how to use a few basic systems. But if you really don't understand what is going on, then either go into business with someone who does, or go on a training course!

Cashflow

A cashflow is simply a projection of your business's income and expenditure. In other words, it is a prediction of when the money is due to come in and go out of your business. Preparing a cashflow and keeping it up to date allows you to budget properly. You can see at a glance when the bills need paying, whether you will need to borrow money, and when you can afford to order materials. Producing a cashflow when you first start in business can be quite difficult, but after a year it becomes easier, as all you need to do is update the figures.

If you intend to borrow from a bank or a funding organisation, one of the first things they will ask for is a cashflow forecast. Figures are usually calculated on a monthly basis. At the end of each month you should update your cashflow by replacing your projections with the actual figures for that month. This constant updating means that keeping the cashflow on a computer spreadsheet is a good idea, as it allows you to change figures easily. Free cashflow forms are available on the internet or from your bank.

Income

Work out how much income you expect from sales and when you expect it to arrive, and enter under "income". Also include here any money received from invoices, fees from other work, VAT collected, and any capital injected e.g. loans. When you are starting up, this is often difficult to estimate, but it is important to have a go, particularly if the business is going to provide your main source of income.

Outgoings

List all the expenses you expect to have to pay each month, and enter them on the sheet under "outgoings". Include your salary, your materials costs, your overheads, and all your other outgoings. You may have different headings than in the example, as everyone's business is different.

Annual forecast

Try to plan your cashflow 12 months in advance; then at the end of each month, fill in the actual figures. Keeping up to date with your cashflow should ensure that you always have enough money to pay the bills when they arrive, and you will know when you can afford to order supplies.

Raising finance

Once you have drawn up a business plan (see chapter 4) and a cashflow projection, you should be able to work out how much capital you will need to start the business, and how much additional funding you will need to finance the cashflow. Raising money needs careful planning, so before you go rushing off to see your bank manager for a loan, check and recheck your figures to make sure that you know exactly how much you need and when you need it.

Your cash requirements will probably be greater at some times of the year than others. You need to plan for times of greatest need, i.e. when you are carrying the greatest amount of stock or waiting for your customers to pay you. Try to steer a middle course – being over-cautious can be as bad as being over-optimistic.

You need money for two purposes:

• Start-up capital

This is the amount of money that you will need to commence in business. It **will include equipment costs, materials, vehicles, premises etc.**

• Working capital

This is your short-term borrowing requirement: the money that will allow you to trade until you are earning sufficient income. It should include an amount to finance the delay between purchasing your materials and selling your product. The amount of money you can raise by borrowing will be limited. If you cannot raise sufficient funds to carry out your plans, they may have to be modified. For instance, you could start on a smaller scale, or work from home instead of renting premises until your business becomes viable.

Your investors
You

The main investor in your business will be you – after all, you cannot expect anyone else to lend you money if you are not prepared to invest yourself. This can be difficult if, for instance, you have just left college and are short of funds. In this case you may have to obtain alternative work until you can raise some capital. If you are expecting anyone else to invest money, the most you can expect is 2 or 3 times the size of your own investment. Examine your own financial position carefully. You may have spare cash in the building society or have possessions you can sell; perhaps you could trade down your car? Starting a business demands sacrifices, and you cannot expect anyone else to take a risk if you aren't prepared to.

Friends and relatives

The most common way of raising finance is to borrow from your family or friends. This source of funding is very useful but should be treated with great caution, as they may need their money back suddenly and you can then be forced into a difficult situation. You must also prepare for what you will do if the business fails and you need to repay your backers. Would you, for example, be able to move house and release some capital?

A loan from friends or relatives could be:

- an interest-free loan – only your nearest and dearest are likely to offer you this. It will probably be short-term, i.e. paid back within months rather than years.
- a loan with interest – to avoid disagreement, fix the interest charges when you start. Use an average over the last six months of the bank base rate. This will probably work out cheaper than a loan from the bank or building society.

Sleeping partner

A partner will need to be aware of your business activities, and they should also be aware of their liability for any debts. Although they are unlikely to be concerned with the day-to-day running of the business, they will certainly want to keep in touch with the way it is run. They will not draw a wage, but will be entitled to a percentage of the profits proportional to their investment.

Grants

You may be able to obtain grants, allowances, cheap loans or awards from a variety of sources. Your first point of contact should be www.gov.uk/business-finance-support-finder, which lists all the current funding available.

If you are prepared to relocate, look at what is available in other areas. For instance, Birmingham has an excellent record for encouraging and supporting small businesses. If you are between the ages of 18 and 30 and unemployed, the Prince's Trust Enterprise Programme offers loans if you cannot raise the finance from other sources, and the Shell LiveWIRE scheme offers similar help.

Bank loans

Borrowing money is expensive, so be careful to work out the best way for your needs. Also consider the financial markets when negotiating a loan. A fixed interest rate loan is good when interest rates are low, but can be a millstone when rates are high and then fall.

Business overdraft

If your need for money is likely to be fairly short-term, an overdraft or short-term loan is likely to be your best option. Overdrafts are flexible and relatively cheap to arrange, but they will only cover part of your financial requirements. The bank may require some type of security, usually in the form of a personal guarantee. Most businesses operate with some type of overdraft facility, but make sure that you agree a limit with the bank and stick to it, as unagreed overdrafts are generally very expensive. The main advantage of an overdraft is that you do not pay interest when you do not use it. The disadvantages are that the interest rate is variable and the bank can demand repayment instantly.

Choosing a bank

There is a lot of help available for businesses from financial institutions and business advisers, all of whom are competing for your custom. Most banks offer some incentive to win your custom. Free banking for a year is a common one, but make sure that the bank is one you will want to be with long-term, as changing banks can involve a lot of paperwork.

Increasingly, financial assistance from banks is being tied to training; for instance currently, at least one high street bank offers free banking for 18 months if you have been on a business training course run by a recognised training agency. This can save you a lot of money in bank charges, so it is worth investigating.

Types of account

Most businesses operate with two types of account:

Business account – these generally offer a full range of banking services including cheque books, paying-in books, monthly statements, standing orders, direct debits, online banking and various types of service card. Do not be tempted to think that you can run a business using a personal account; you will not be able to obtain any credit references, which will be essential as your business grows. When you are starting up you should be able to find free banking of some sort.

Reserve account – these are instant-access accounts to which you can transfer your spare cash to accumulate interest. The interest rate that they pay is usually fairly minimal, so if you do have large amounts of cash spare, it will probably be better off in a building society.

TOP TIP

Before embarking on a business, carry out a personal survival budget so you know how much you need to earn to pay your living costs.

Credit Cards

The majority of people now expect to have the option of paying by credit card whether they are at a Craft Fair or Art Exhibition. Failure to take these payments may mean that you will lose sales.

There are various methods of taking payments at fairs depending on your IT equipment. Check with your bank or business association if they offer any deals for mobile transactions. One popular method is using iZettle. This can be used with a number of phones and tablets including the Ipad or Iphone. You pay a one off fee and then a percentage of the sale. The customer receives their receipt by email.

CHAPTER 11

Your Suppliers

inding suppliers is so much easier than it used to be, with the help of the Internet. Along with the benefits there are some problems, however – a lot of supplies now come in from abroad, and are not repeatable – you might have a very popular line in baby blankets, for example, but when you try and reorder the fabric you might find it's no longer available. You may need a wholesaler, too; these can be more difficult to find, as they do not always have a strong Internet presence.

The importance of the right supplier

Finding good suppliers for your materials is vital if you want to build a business. Whether it is fabric, clay or silver, buying at the right price can make the difference between success and failure. Magazines such as Craft and Design, Crafts and Ceramics Review can be a good sources of knowledge, and a selection of products are available on websites such as Etsy; but do shop around. For some products you may need to source a specialist supplier.

Ebay

In recent years, ebay has taken over as one of the main suppliers of materials for craftworkers and artists. Often supplying in small quantities, the site can prove invaluable when trying out new materials. It is also a good place to sell your surplus materials. Many creative people earn part of their income by selling materials over the site. By buying in large quantities and then selling your surplus over ebay you can increase your income.

TOP TIP
Cutting the cost of your supplies will make your business more profitable. It is always worth spending time searching for and securing the best price.

Local retailers
If you are just starting up, you may find that local retailers where you can buy in small quantities are best. If you are a regular customer, it is fine to ask if they do a discount. Some of these retailers also have a web presence with a trade section, which will be worth a look.

Using an Internet search engine
On the Internet you can use your search engine (e.g. Google) to find what you need. For instance if you are looking for beads, think of words associated with beads (e.g. beads, glass, vintage, silver, ceramic, wholesale, trade). Type two or three of these words in and see what comes up. You may have to do several searches to get a good result.

Finding a wholesaler
Thumbing through your dog-eared Yellow Pages or calling a directory service might seem old fashioned, but a lot of wholesalers still rely on these traditional methods. If you live in a large city such as Manchester or London you might find an area where many wholesalers are located, and it may be simply a matter of taking your business credentials, business card, etc. and calling in at some until you find what you want. Initially they will probably want you to pay upfront either with cash or a credit card, so be prepared.

Relationships between wholesalers and their customers are often built up over years of loyal service, so suppliers rely on word of mouth and local knowledge to attract new clients. Wholesalers rarely advertise, but there is a publication called The Trader, which you might find useful, this is available from newsagents, or online at www.thetrader.co.uk.

Searching for suppliers at trade shows

Trade shows and exhibitions are among the best places to network, establish rapport with potential clients, and find new suppliers. Fairs attract exhibitors and visitors from around the world, and afford a prime opportunity to see what's out there. To find the appropriate fairs and expos, it's worth checking trade publications associated with your sector, and you should have a look at websites such as www.exhibitions.co.uk or www.tradeshows.esources.co.uk

You should ensure that the trade fair you attend is relevant to your needs, as attending can be quite costly. The largest trade fair in the UK is Spring Fair, held in February each year at the NEC in Birmingham.

Most trade fairs have websites, and it's usually possible to check which wholesale distributors and suppliers will be present. If you can't find relevant details online, it's worth asking the trade show management for a list of vendors and attendees, so you can have an idea of which suppliers you'd like to connect with before the day itself.

Network with other makers, and you might be able to order in larger quantities and get bigger discounts. And always have back-up suppliers – sometimes they go bust!

Continuity of Supply

If you buy materials regularly always make sure you purchase sufficient. There is nothing more frustrating than having a good selling line and not being able to repeat the fabric or beads. Check before purchasing if it's a stock line or likely to disappear.

TOP TIP

If you are prepared to demonstrate or write articles about products, suppliers may provide you with samples free of charge.

CHAPTER 12
Legal matters

Copyright

Copying is unfortunately common in the creative industries, and as soon as your work starts appearing on the shelves you are vulnerable to someone else who has more money and more outlets copying your designs and producing ranges, which are very similar. It therefore makes sense to protect your work a much as possible. This is particularly important when you start exhibiting at trade shows or marketing your work online.

How to protect yourself

There are various organisations that offer copyright protection, the main ones being ACID (Anti-Copying In Design, www.acid.uk.com) and the Gift Association's scheme Copywatch (www.ga-uk.org). If you belong to one of these, always display their symbol on your publicity material so people know your work is protected. Alternatively you could take out an insurance policy to protect you. Find a law firm with a specialist in IPR (Intellectual Property Rights).

Prevention is better than cure

- Adopt a document and management system by keeping signed and dated records of all initial designs – ask a friend to sign or witness them. Record each stage of the design process.
- Keep photographic records, either use the date function on the camera, or email them to yourself. It is possible to register products before you put them on display at a trade show on the Registers Community but it is expensive and probably only worth doing if your work is really unique.
- Always use the copyright symbol on your products, and if registered give the design register and the number.
- Keep records of when and where the work first went on sale.
- At fairs, be wary of people with mobile phones and cameras or even sketchpads. You can put up a notice saying "no photographs".
- Don't forget that it is possible for two people to have the same idea at the same time, particularly if it is fashionable or reflects a current event, so check that no one else is producing similar designs.
- Always state the following on invoices and order forms, and on your website: "All intellectual property rights in our designs are and will remain the property of (your name). Any infringement of these rights will be pursued rigorously."

Top tip

If you think you are being copied, don't tackle the copier straight off: try to get proof. Obtain copies of their catalogue or print off pages from their website.

Health and safety

Wherever you work, you are responsible for making sure that the workplace is safe and secure. If you employ more than 5 people, you need to have a Health and Safety policy in place. See www.hse.gov.uk for further information.

Legal documents

NEVER sign a legal document without having a solicitor look at it. It will cost money, but it could save you a lot more money in the future. Many solicitors have a fixed-price fee for new clients, so ask around before booking an appointment.

Part 3

Finding your customers

CHAPTER 13

You and your customers

No one can survive in business without customers. These are the people who give you money for your product or service, and they need to be treated properly. Your customers can range from people making one-off purchases, to collectors who buy from you regularly. Most creatives will sell their work to several different types of customer: individuals, curators, and businesses. Whoever you are trying to sell your work to, it is important to understand why they buy. To do this, you need to find out as much about them as possible. Anyone can buy your work, but you cannot make for everyone – if you have someone in mind when you make your work you will have a better chance of selling.

Identifying your customers

When you are producing a piece of work, whether it is a necklace or a painting, ask yourself, **"who is going to pay for this?"** That person is your customer. If you cannot imagine someone else paying for the work, then you are paying for it. If you have not yet started selling, you may find it hard to imagine your customers; but it is important to try. Consider what they look like, where they live, what else they buy, etc. You can do this in a number of ways:

Visual picture – buy a magazine of the type you think your customer would purchase, cut out images, which reflect your customer, and create a collage. Put this in a prominent place, to remind you who you are making for.

Word association – try describing your customer in just a couple of phrases. The following descriptions could be applied to different types of customers who would buy different products:

- Rich and rustic
- Budget-conscious with exotic tastes
- Modern and mobile

If you know who your customers are, it makes everything you do more effective. You can target your advertising more effectively, and go to fairs where your customers are likely to visit. Your work can grow with your customers – if you are targeting the student market, you can decide to stay with that, or you can move with your customers when they start to settle down and their tastes and needs alter. If your customers live in large loft apartments then you can size your artwork accordingly.

You may attract different customers if you produce a number of ranges, but beware of trying to be all things to all people. And don't expect all your customers to fit your profile; there will always be exceptions, but to be a success you need to produce for the majority, not the exception.

When you have a clear idea of your customer, you will become aware of the limitations of your market. For example, if you are designing lampshades suitable for an interior designer to use in wine bars, you will clearly have a limited market; so if you can also design a range suitable for selling to individuals, you will target a different market and increase your chances of success.

Customer care

Many creatives worry that they are not very good at selling. Crafts and artwork are not like double-glazing – the "hard sell" is unlikely to be necessary, and in fact can be counter-productive. Treat your customers properly, and if you are making the right product at the right price, they will buy. Customers need to feel valued, so be friendly, show them appreciation, and they will return.

Twelve rules for customer care

- Smile every time you greet a customer.
- Never ignore customers – speak to them, or reply to their emails, as soon as possible.
- Always apologise for a delay.
- Never talk to a friend rather than to a customer.
- If you cannot help, suggest someone who can.
- Never leave a customer to answer the phone – use an answerphone, or let your mobile go to voicemail.
- Never criticise one customer to another.
- Don't react if the customer is less than complimentary; they might just be having a bad day.
- Don't let it show if you don't like a customer. Many creatives are very proprietorial about their work and only like it to go to good homes – don't fall into this trap!
- If you want information, ask politely: manners cost nothing.
- Address customers by name if possible.
- Everyone likes a gift: a free key-ring from a leatherworker or even a free pen with your name and number on it will be appreciated.

TOP TIP
if you are taking the details of a customer you know but whose name you have forgotten, ask them for their surname and they will generally give you their full name.

Creating a customer database
Building and using a customer database is one of the most useful marketing tools for all artists and craftworkers. A computer is the ideal way to store

a database; there are several free software packages available for managing a customer database, or you could just use Microsoft Access or even Excel. It is also possible to keep a database on a card index system. The uses to which you could put your database are:

- to inform customers which craft fairs you are attending
- to inform them of exhibitions
- to tell them about new products
- to tell them of your successes e.g. awards or competitions.

Note that if you keep your mailing list on a computer, you may need to register with the Data Protection Act. For further information on this, go to http://ico.org.uk Always ensure you hold information securely, for instance by password-protecting your database.

Building a mailing list

Start collecting names and addresses as soon as possible. You'll need to ask permission, but people are generally happy to let you write to them. As postage is so expensive you will probably prefer to contact them by email. The most useful people to have on your list are:

- people who have bought from you in the past
- potential customers - those that have made enquires, but not yet placed an order
- media contacts
- members of arts associations
- gallery owners (you can use Yellow Pages, online directories, or publications from the Arts Council etc. to find addresses)

If you don't have a mailing list, you can buy one; but you can only use it once, and it is unlikely to be as effective as one you've built yourself.

How to acquire the names

- When you make a sale, always ask the customer for their name and contact details. Occasionally someone might refuse, but not often.
- Have a clipboard on your stall for people to put their names on if they want you to send them details. If you make it clear that you will not sell or pass the information on to anyone else, then people are usually quite happy to add their names and email addresses.
- When attending any function or trade fair, always ask people for a business card; this can be added to your list of contacts.

When you have compiled a list, do use it! Email is cheaper than post; but emails are easily deleted whereas an attractive postcard can be kept for years, so use a mixture of both methods if possible.

TOP TIP

Groups of artists and makers can pool their resources and do a joint mailing to save money.

Newsletters

Newsletters can be a very effective means of promotion, providing a link between you and your customer. They can be used to advertise your presence at shows, to launch new products, or to remind customers of your range. Newsletters are relatively inexpensive to produce and can be distributed to your mailing list by post or email, given to customers at craft fairs, and included with orders.

Include personal information if you enjoy having a social relationship with your customers. Many of them become friends over the years, and like to keep in touch. Some of the best newsletters involve the customers in the business by sharing details that they wouldn't have otherwise known.

Producing a newsletter

Desktop publishing and cheap digital printing have made it easy to produce professional-looking newsletters at low cost. If possible, use slightly heavier paper than is usually available; it does make a difference, and costs very little extra. If sending electronically, consider using MailChimp www.mailchimp. com or a similar system.

Use illustrations where possible. Scan in a drawing or photo, use stock images or copyright-free clip art, or if all else fails, print out your newsletter and paste an illustration on before photocopying it.

Newsletters are most effective if produced on a regular basis. Every three months is a good interval, unless you have something special to announce sooner. You can include special offers, discount vouchers, or even carry advertising for fellow creatives to help with the cost. Details of interesting commissions, exhibitions, prizes won or the use of new materials are all of interest to your customers. If you find it difficult to think of something to write, think of the type of questions you are asked at craft fairs; this is the type of information that is most likely to appeal to your readers.

CHAPTER 14

Craft fairs and farmers' markets

One of the main outlets for craftwork is through craft fairs. These vary greatly in their size, quality and ability to draw customers. The Crafts Council and Craft and Design magazine both have lists of craft fairs and exhibiting opportunities. Also look out for details in local libraries or carry out an Internet search.

Finding a fair

Fairs vary widely in quality and size; you must choose carefully, and target your market in exactly the same way as if you were selling to shops. Sometimes fairs, which are billed as "craft fairs" actually allow people to sell bought-in goods – this causes concern within the industry and creates problems for the genuine craftworker. A fair that is really successful one year may be a disaster the next, for reasons ranging from the weather, to the fact that a new attraction has been sited in the area. Also, many small craft fair organiser's start up at venues that are too small or far away from the centres of population, and fail to attract sufficient customers.

It is essential to visit as many craft fairs as possible before deciding where you want to exhibit. Talk to the stallholders who are already exhibiting: they are usually very helpful. Watch what people are buying. Do the customers match your customer profile?

You also need to remember that many craft fairs book up 12 months in advance, so it may take time to get into the one you want. Most successful craftworkers book all their fairs in January so they can plan their production.

Craft fair organisers

Different organisers run the various events around the country; some are national events, and others are mainly local. You will probably want to start locally and find your feet; but do avoid the amateur craft fair, which is unlikely to attract the type of customer you require. Go to a fair organised by one of the recognised organisers listed in the publications mentioned above. The experience that you will gain at that first fair will be invaluable, even if sales are lower than you hoped.

How to apply for a stand

Having decided which shows you want to apply for, write to or email the organisers and ask for details and a list of venues. Some organisers request an S.A.E. for information and a booking form. A good organiser will usually ask to see samples of your work; at the very least they should ask to see photographs (make sure yours are good quality and well-lit), or for details of where you have previously exhibited. They may ask for a link to your website: this is an increasingly popular method of judging people's work.

Professional organisers want to present as good as show as possible; if they turn you down, try to find out why. They should also provide a wide variety of crafts at each show, so if they refuse you at one show they may well offer you an alternative venue.

When filling in the forms, read the terms and conditions carefully. These should include details of:

- what happens in the event of a show being cancelled
- what happens if you cancel your stall
- fire safety regulations

- insurance requirements
- when you can set up and take down
- any details about demonstrating

What are crafts?

There is much debate about craft fairs, which allow the resale of bought- in goods. Most craft fair organisers will state that they do not allow this, but if they have last-minute cancellations or poor bookings they are often tempted to allow this type of trader in rather than have an empty space. Organisers maintain that this is better for everyone's sake, and preferable to cancelling the show. It can however be very frustrating, if you are selling real craftwork, to be placed next to someone selling cheap imported goods. There is little you can do about it except to avoid those organisers in the future. You can help the organisers by not cancelling your stall at the last minute because you haven't enough products – this is a frequent complaint of organisers, particularly during the Christmas period.

TOP TIP

If you are unsure how much stock you need for a craft fair, a general rule of thumb is ten times the rent of the stand. So if the stand costs £100, you will need £1,000 worth of stock. Experience will show whether this ratio works for you.

Cost of a stall

Generally space is booked in units of 6ft x 2ft tables (about 1.8m x 0.6m). A basic 6ft table can cost anything from £20 to £200+ for a day depending on venue, number of customers expected, etc. Obviously what you receive for £100 will be more than you will get for £20; if you want to exhibit at a top venue with tens of thousands of visitors then you will need to be prepared to pay for the privilege. Initially rents might seem high, but two days' rent of a craft stall may be equivalent in sales to a week's shop rent and council tax. Remember, if the organisers do not charge sufficient rent, they will not have the money to advertise widely and promote the event properly.

What do you get for the money?

The stand fee will normally include the hire of a 6ft x 2ft table, two chairs, and a power supply for lights. Sometimes electricity is charged as an extra, so check this; occasionally it may not even be supplied at all.

If there is the opportunity to advertise in a brochure, make sure you supply the necessary information in time for publication. Similarly if you want to demonstrate, make sure that you will be allowed to, and that you will have enough room. Some organisers encourage demonstrations and will allow you more space or give you some free publicity.

Before the show

A good organiser will supply you with all the necessary information about setting-up times, opening times for the public, how to reach the venue, unloading, and parking arrangements. This is particularly important at city venues – at shows like Chelsea you have very little time to unload, and everything is timed to precision. Don't forget to book accommodation in plenty of time. If it's outside term time, student accommodation can be a good option. Some events have caravan or camping sites attached. Don't forget that you will have a van or car full of stock, so choose somewhere with secure parking.

The organiser may also send you some publicity material to distribute. Use it! The more visitors that arrive, the greater your chance of success.

Insurance

Most event organisers require you to have public liability insurance. Sometimes they will include a form for insurance when you apply for a stand. It is important to be properly insured at events, and to ensure that your goods are insured when being transported or if stored in your van overnight. Artists' News (www.a-n.co.uk) offers £5million public liability insurance included in membership to practicing artists, The SAA (Society for All Artists) also offers insurance, and some guilds and associations have joint policies, which are good value.

At the show

There should be a plan displayed giving details of your stand, or there may be someone to greet you or book you in. It will often appear chaotic and confusing to the beginner, so if you are not sure, ask; don't worry about being the newcomer, as everyone has to start somewhere.

Your stand

The standards of display seen at craft fairs are increasingly professional. Basic etiquette demands that your table is covered on three sides and that none of the boxes etc. can be seen, but if you want to make an impact you will have to go further than this. See Chapter 6 on display for some ideas.

Don't block access to your neighbours' stands or try to take over their areas; this really will cause problems. Make sure your stand is ready to go, with all boxes cleared from the gangways, well in advance of opening.

It's always a good idea to take someone with you to help with the loading and unloading and to allow you to have a coffee break. If you must eat on the stand, do it discreetly; the sight of someone munching a sandwich is not the professional image you are aiming for!

During the show

If you have a list of customers, don't forget to let them know that you will be showing at a certain event. Make sure that everything you sell is labeled, and include a price list with all purchases.

Occupy the time - try to do something related to your work rather than read the paper. Always smile and greet potential customers. And remember that your appearance matters as well. No one expects a collar and tie (unless of course you make ties!) but your appearance should reflect the quality of your products.

After the show

Even if you are having a slow day, don't be tempted to clear up before the show ends – this will incur the wrath of the organisers, make you look unprofessional, and might make you miss a last-minute sale.

Follow up on enquiries as soon as possible, and add any new names and addresses to your database and mailing list. Keep records of all the shows you attend, how much you took, what sold well and what you could have sold. Over a period of time these records will enable you to build up a picture of patterns of trading, and which events provide the best results.

TOP TIP
smile, smile, smile!

CHAPTER 15

Supplying the trade

Some creatives gain their initial experience of selling by exhibiting at craft fairs or by selling from their studio. For some, especially those who enjoy the lifestyle of the craft fair circuit, this provides sufficient income and a market for all their production. For others, who want to grow their business and enjoy the experience of seeing their work sold in retail outlets, there are various ways of approaching the retail market. You can visit retailers yourself or employ an agent, but exhibiting at a trade show can be the most cost-effective way of reaching trade customers.

Finding galleries/shops

To begin your search, write down a list of all the galleries/retailers where you think your work would sell; check the Yellow Pages, the Internet, and gallery guides for ideas. Make a list of 20 possible retailers to review in person. If you are trying to target another area of the country then you might have to plan a holiday around your visits.

When you visit the galleries/shops, you need to collect as much information as you can. Have a small notebook and jot things down as soon as you leave the premises. If they hold exhibitions, ask for a list and to be put on their mailing list. Ask yourself the following questions.

- Do they stock similar work to mine? You may feel you have found a gap in the market, but most galleries know their customers. If they stock traditional watercolours then that is what their customers want, not abstract artwork.
- Are the price points similar? If they only stock mass-produced jewellery then your designer range might not fit in.
- Are the goods or paintings displayed properly?

Approaching a gallery or shop

If you have a product, which you think is suitable to sell in a gallery or shop, there is nothing to stop you approaching the retailer direct. Initially it is a good idea to call in and leave a brochure or card, and ask for an appointment. If they don't contact you, it's fine to follow up with a phone call, but don't hassle them; retailers know what sells for them, and your product might not be right for them. Alternatively you can approach them by email initially, but if they don't recognise your name, you may easily end up in the trash box.

Once you have made contact, some galleries will ask you to send images by email; others will set up appointments. Galleries are increasingly asking for details of your website and deciding whether to look at your work based on that; so make sure your website is up-to-date and shows your best work.

When visiting a gallery, if your product is portable there is no harm in having it with you and (if the staff aren't busy) asking for their opinion to see if it is suitable for their market.

If you get an appointment

Go prepared! The three main complaints of gallery owners are that artists arrive unprepared; bring inappropriate/unfinished work; and fail to deliver on time. Don't be guilty of these! Always arrive early so you can be relaxed.

Take with you:

- Portfolio/CV and photos of your work (with original reviews, exhibit announcements, etc.)
- Price list
- Several perfect pieces of your original work.

If you are rejected, ask them if they can suggest another gallery/ shop. They might tell you that you are not ready; listen carefully to any advice. Keep records of everyone you have seen and how the interview went.

Fine art galleries

Fine art galleries vary from community-based, not-for-profit galleries to upmarket galleries in large cities like London. Local galleries often exist to promote local artists, and can be a great place to start. Some gallery owners also act as agents and will represent artists, but they mostly prefer established artists who have started to develop a collector base.

A good way to start researching potential outlets for your work is by visiting other artists' exhibitions and previews. Networking is important in any business, and particularly in the art world. Don't dismiss going abroad: the German market for artwork is particularly strong.

Remember, you do not need to live in an area to exhibit there. If you want to build a career as a fine artist, you should do your research and be prepared to travel to suitable galleries to show them your work

Steps to approaching a gallery

- *Call and ask to speak to the owner, or whoever selects the work.*
- *Tell them that you have visited the gallery and that you think your work is appropriate.*
- *Ask for an appointment to show your portfolio/ samples.*
- *If this fails, ask if you can send them some information. Ask if they have a preference about the format – they might prefer email, with attachments in a particular format such as TIFF or jpeg. Always make sure you get a contact name.*
- *You can also email a link to your website.*
- *Note that many galleries receive hundreds of emails a week; so if they don't specify that they only want email, it might be more*

> *memorable to send your images as postcards with details about you and your website.*
> - *Give the gallery four weeks to review your work. If they have not called or returned the work by then, telephone them and ask if they want any more information; but don't harass them.*

Exhibiting at a trade show

One good way of bringing your work to the attention of a lot of retailers is to exhibit at a trade show. Opportunities to exhibit at trade fairs have never been greater; there are an ever-increasing number of fairs both in the UK and in Europe. However, before you embark on this route you need to ask yourself the following questions:

- Do I have the financial capacity to handle increased sales? Trade customers will want credit, and if you are under-capitalized and receive a lot of orders you could end up with cashflow problems.
- What are my production levels? Can I produce enough extra stock to warrant the cost of taking a stand, and can I deliver the goods on time?
- Will my suppliers be able to meet my increased demand for raw materials?
- Do I have the space to hold the extra stock necessary?
- Can I "sell" my work to trade buyers? This needs a different approach from craft fairs.
- Will my work travel, or will the cost of carriage be prohibitive?

Having decided that you have the ability to exhibit at trade fairs, the next step is to identify which show is right for you. Always visit the show before you exhibit, and talk to the other exhibitors and the organisers. You will need to decide whether you are going to exhibit alone or with a group. In the case of some of the bigger fairs, which have waiting lists, the only way you can exhibit is by joining a group stand. The best of these jury the products to ensure a consistently high standard, which does attract the buyers.

Selecting a show

Your choice of show will depend on availability and on what you want to achieve: if you are looking for export orders you may choose one fair, and if you are looking for orders from department stores, you will choose another. Contact the organisers of the shows that you are interested in and ask for an exhibitor's pack. Some shows offer a new exhibitor package, or special discounts for new exhibitors. The pack should provide you with the following information:

- Buyers – the number and type of buyers, whether they are from multiples, gallery owners, overseas. Are the people they sell to, your potential customers?
- Awards – are there any awards, any opportunities for promotion?
- Reputation – how long has the show been going? Which organisation sponsors it?
- Cost – what do the costs include? Is electricity included in the package? When budgeting, don't forget to allow for the cost of your display stand and lighting, and include travel and accommodation costs.
- Restrictions – are there restrictions on what you can exhibit? Are there limits on stand type, stand height, number of personnel, and use of models, music, or demonstrations?
- Timing – does the show fit into your schedule or does it compete with other shows? If you are going to be taking Christmas orders, will it give you enough time to produce them?

The shows

Trade shows change from year to year as new halls are added or the product emphasis is changed. Check out the current state of the fairs below.

The British Craft Trade Fair www.bctf.co.uk

The UK's only specialist craft trade fair is held each year in Harrogate. It provides a good starting place and attracts mainly gallery and independent buyers. It offers a special deal for newcomers, which is a cost-effective way to test the market.

Spring Fair International, Birmingham www.springfair.com

Billed as the largest gift fair in Europe, the only way for a newcomer to exhibit here will probably be on a group stand or by joining a long waiting list. With such a large fair it is important to be in the right place, or the buyers will miss you. It is now divided into specialist sections, which may or may not work to your advantage depending on the type of work you produce. This fair also has a section for fine art. It is mainly the commercial galleries, but if you think your work will reproduce well as prints, visit on the last day of the show with a small portfolio and talk to some of the people on the stands.

Autumn Fair International, Birmingham www.autumnfair.com

This is the younger of the TPS fairs. It is well placed for orders for the profitable Christmas period as long as you can meet the demand. It has made an effort to attract design-led exhibitors in recent years.

Top Drawer, London www.topdrawer.co.uk

This fair is held twice a year, in spring and autumn. These shows have large design-led sections and attract a lot of export buyers.

Booking space

Some spaces are definitely better than others; but as most shows book space on a seniority system, it may be a while before you get one of the better spaces, and you may have to take what is available in the first year. Once you have started exhibiting, don't be afraid to ask for a better position. You can compensate to some extent for a poor position by making the best use of the space and inviting as many buyers as possible to the show. If you make the right choice in the first place and stay for a few years then you should get a good pitch.

Group stands

For craftworkers, particularly those starting out, an increasingly popular option is the group stand. These vary in their type, and are usually organised by regional groups such as Made in Cumbria. A general group is DesignGAP, designgap.co.uk, who book a block of stalls, which craftworkers can apply for. These organisations are trying to present the best, so you must expect your work to be juried. Some group stands operate on the 'by invitation only' principle. Working on a group stand can be difficult – people usually operate a rota system for manning the stand, but some people find it difficult to sell other people's work.

How to have a successful show

You can have a significant impact on the success of your show by taking a professional approach.

12 golden rules for a successful show:

- Read the exhibitor's handbook thoroughly and make sure you have ordered everything you need.
- Rent one of the Video Arts (www.videoarts.com) training videos on successful exhibiting, start designing your stand as soon as possible, and have a trial run.
- Reaching the hall can take ages at some venues, so arrive in good time, allowing as long as possible to erect your stand.
- Organise reliable help for the show, and make sure that they are fully briefed on your business. It is not acceptable at a trade show to ask next- door to keep an eye on your stand! You may also have a considerable distance to transport your goods, so you'll need help.
- Make sure that you not only have that vital order book on your stand, but also a book for potential leads, business cards, etc.
- Don't build a barrier between you and your customers. They should be able to get onto your stand easily.

- Remember that trade buyers will wonder how your products will look in their shops, so pay particular attention to your display, which should be as interesting as possible and feature point-of-sale display material.
- Highlight new products and any awards you have won. The words "new" and "success" are very powerful, so use them in your publicity.
- It is unlikely that you can demonstrate at a trade fair, but you can have photographs of yourself in your studio.
- If posters and photographs can enhance your exhibits then use large ones, and make sure that they are professionally produced.
- You could offer a special deal available only at the show to encourage buyers.
- Don't worry too much if you don't achieve the orders you expected. Buyers often like time to consider new products, and sometimes you may have to wait until the second year.

Follow-up

After the show, contact all the buyers who left their card. Following up the leads from a show can often be the most important part of exhibiting.

CHAPTER 16

Organising an exhibition

Arranging an exhibition of your work is not as difficult as it may first appear. Sometimes people refuse offers of exhibition because they are not sure what is expected of them and whether they can cope, yet it can be a very rewarding and exciting experience. Exhibitions can be the work of one person or a group. Sometimes the combination of work by two artists, such as a fine artist and a potter, can work to the benefit of both of them.

It is important to decide exactly why you want an exhibition. There are five main reasons for exhibiting your work:

- To show your work to the public. Creative work needs to be seen by people in order to give it meaning, and most makers value this contact with a wider audience.
- To give you the opportunity to see your work displayed in its entirety, in good, well lit surroundings, which show it off to best advantage.

- To establish your reputation as an artist or craftworker, and to introduce yourself to fellow creatives other exhibition organisers, galleries and collectors.
- To sell your work and obtain commissions. You will obviously need to cover the costs of preparing the exhibition but you will also want to make some money.
- To provide a focus for your working life. Having an exhibition can be wonderfully motivating.

Possible venues

There are a surprising number of places prepared to exhibit artwork. Some offer their facilities free, while others charge or take a commission. Always remember that you put a lot of work into an exhibition and you want as many people as possible to see it, so a good location is the main priority. The following list of venues should give you some idea of the type of places available. Some venues don't allow you to sell; don't dismiss these out of hand, as they might lead to increased business provided the work is clearly identified and people can contact you easily. Some venues put restrictions on the type of work displayed: for example some charitable organisations will not display items, which they consider to be against their aims.

Most venues that have regular exhibitions will have agreement forms for you to sign; only you can decide whether the terms are suitable but if the agreement is very complicated and difficult to understand, check with a solicitor before signing.

• Studio Exhibitions

When finding a venue to exhibit your work, look first at what you already have available. If your studio is small, cramped and at the back of beyond it is probably not a good place to hold an exhibition; but if you or a friend live in a converted barn or other interesting property you might find holding an exhibition there will attract more people than a traditional gallery, particularly as most people love to look round someone else's home. You will need to check if you require any type of planning permission but it is unlikely for a short-term exhibition.

• Cafes and restaurants

Don't dismiss cafes and restaurants; they can be great places to exhibit. If they have a regular clientele, change your work regularly so it keeps looking fresh. Watch your price points – people out for a meal are unlikely to pay thousands of pounds for a painting. However, it is a good way to get established, and you never know which curators or art collectors are eating there! Make sure you leave plenty of business cards and call in regularly. If the owner spots someone who likes your work they will introduce you.

• Building society/bank windows

Window space on a high street can be very valuable. Any sort of business that does not serve the retail trade may make their windows available. It may help if you are a customer; otherwise try to fit in with a local festival or Christmas, when they may be looking for a way of decorating their window. Approach the manager, and be prepared to leave samples of your work and publicity material, as they may have to check with their head office.

• Local authority galleries

Many local authorities and some of the smaller tourist attractions have gallery space at reasonable prices, although this often gets booked up well in advance. Enterprise Agencies, Tourist Information Centres and business organisations may have display space for local work, or may use your work to decorate a stand at an exhibition. They often find it difficult to find attractive products made locally, particularly in areas where heavy industry or service industries predominate, so it is always worth making them aware of your work. This can also lead to corporate commissions.

• Private galleries

Private or commercial galleries are the most commonly used venues for exhibitions. Check with the owner regarding their exhibitions policy. They generally like to nurture artists over the long-term, but they sometimes also have specialist exhibitions when they exhibit work by a variety of makers or artists, and you may be able to be included in this type of exhibition.

• Showcases

Showcases are available in large hotels, corporate buildings etc. They can prove a useful place for exposure, particularly if you work to commission rather than selling individual items.

• Foyers

Foyers of theatres, concert halls, etc. are increasingly being used for this type of exhibition to provide an added attraction for their customers.

• Libraries/tourist Information centres

Libraries and Tourist Information centres often have a room, which is used for exhibitions. The cost is usually more reasonable than the commercial galleries. You may be surprised by the results, as these venues attract a wide variety of people.

• Other spaces

Craftworkers at Manchester Craft Centre noticed an increase in the number of visitors since their work was on display at Manchester Airport, not a traditional place for craftworkers to exhibit. If you are imaginative you might be able to think of other such venues.

Approaching a gallery

It is generally a waste of time trying to persuade a gallery owner to exhibit work totally different from their usual format, so look for galleries, which normally exhibit work similar to yours. Your local Arts Council may have details of exhibition spaces. Most local authorities now have Arts Officers who may offer assistance; and you could look at advertisements for other exhibitions in your local paper to identify potential venues. Remember that popular venues get booked up well in advance, sometimes two or three years ahead. You could always ask if there is anyone with an exhibition already booked who may be willing to share the exhibition space.

Working out a budget

The cost of holding an exhibition should not be underestimated, and this is why it is often sensible initially to share an exhibition with others. Before you agree to an exhibition, sit down and work out the costs. These will include:

- Hire of venue – there may be a fixed charge, or the gallery could take a percentage of any sales (this will usually require a guaranteed minimum payment). Find out what the hire of the venue includes: sometimes the gallery will be responsible for the cost of the private view, at other times you will be responsible for everything.

- Catalogue printing – all exhibitions benefit from having a catalogue and these can be expensive to produce, although you may be able to do it yourself if you have the skills. Colour postcards of your main pieces accompanied by a printed price list may be an alternative to a traditional catalogue, particularly useful if you plan to rotate the pieces on display.

- Posters – if you are trying to attract the general public to your show then you may need to print some posters. If you work is particularly collectable you may be able to sell the posters at the exhibition to recover some of the cost.

- Publicity – the amount you need to spend on publicity will depend on who you are trying to attract and the location of the venue. If you are in a high street gallery with good passing trade you may not need a great deal of publicity, but if you are exhibiting in a lesser-known venue you may need to spend a considerable amount to ensure that people visit the exhibition.

- Mailshot – if you already have a customer database you will need to make sure that you send invitations to all these people, in addition to critics, other gallery owners, potential customers and anyone who might stage another exhibition.

- Hire of equipment – not all venues will be able to provide exactly the type of display stands and lighting that you require. It is important that your goods are displayed properly, so allow for the hire of equipment in your budget.

- Cost of private view – most exhibitions hold a private view prior to the opening, when collectors, past customers, friends, relatives, influential people and the press are invited for a glass of wine and some light refreshments. The scale of this will depend on the venue and who you are trying to attract.

- Social media – all forms of social media should be used to advertise the exhibition. If you don't use Twitter yourself, try to get other people to Tweet about it. Put it on Facebook and on as many listings as possible.

Organising an exhibition

- Dates – it is important to time the exhibition as carefully as possible. If you are trying to exhibit in a gallery for the first time, you may have to accept the dates that they offer, and then try to move to a better time the next year.

- Planning the workload – you need to ensure that you will have enough work to show at the exhibition. This can act as a useful discipline for creatives who are not very focused, but can be difficult for those who panic when faced with deadlines. You will also need to allow time for organising the exhibition; a commercial gallery may undertake to do this for you, but you will still have to supply them with customer lists and other information.

- The private view – this is a time when invited individuals can view the work in private, meet the craftworker or artist and hopefully buy before the general public is allowed to view. You need to send a lot more invitations than the number of people you expect to attend. You can obviously rely on friends and family to support you, but critics and potential customers might not be so obliging. Invitations are never wasted – even if people don't come to the private view they may well visit the exhibition at another time.

- Compiling a guest list – ask the venue if they keep a guest list. You should also include:
  - gallery owners
  - local retailers
  - local art college staff
  - art association officials
  - your advisers, such as bank managers
  - friends and family
  - your existing customers
  - local personalities
  - members of the press
  - funders and supporters
  - representatives from craft associations or guilds you belong to
- Display – good display is vital. A poor display will spoil even the best objects. You do not need to spend a lot of money on expensive display items – care and attention to detail are more important – but don't compromise on good lighting. Check the display regularly throughout the exhibition. Provide professional-looking labels; either use a computer or ask a friend who does calligraphy to help. Labels should include the maker's name, the date of making, details of the process, the catalogue number if used, and the selling price. If you are borrowing back any items specifically for the exhibition, remember to credit the owner and state clearly that the items are on loan.
- Insurance – if the venue does not provide insurance, make sure that you are covered under your own policy, or take out additional cover.
- Title – choosing a good exhibition title is important. Don't assume that people know your work. "Ceramics by Chris Smith" immediately tells people what is on display. "New Work by Chris Smith" does not.
- Posters – printed posters are expensive but effective; if you can design your own and use a local print shop this will cut costs. Before deciding on the size of posters think about where you intend to display them, as many places will only accept A4 size, and offering larger ones is a waste of time.

- Advertisements – the venue should publicise your exhibition in their literature and on their website. An advertisement in your local paper will probably be sufficient in terms of press advertisements; you may be able to do this jointly with the venue.
- Press releases – these are very important. They should be sent to all the local press, local radio etc. See Chapter 24, "Public relations", for advice on writing a good press release.
- Mailshots – if you keep a customer list, then you need to mailshot them, either by post or by email. For a large or first exhibition, you might consider purchasing a mailing list. Don't forget to put a visitors' book on display and/or a box for business cards, as this will enable you to build a list of interested people for future exhibitions.
- The catalogue – a catalogue is basically a list of the products in the exhibition, although it can be much more. It should have details about you, your background, and your previous exhibitions and commissions. You could consider having a general brochure printed, and using an insert listing the exhibits at each exhibition. Colour postcards are good publicity items, which people can take home to remind them of your work; attractive cards like these are often kept and pinned on boards, keeping your work in focus.

TOP TIP

if you know someone who is good at curating exhibitions, ask for their help. Hanging an exhibition well is a skill, and a good curator can make all the difference.

Exhibiting at short notice

Sometimes opportunities arise for you to exhibit at short notice. It may seem a wonderful opportunity, but if you don't have your best work available or have to rush your work, be very wary. A badly prepared exhibition, with insufficient work on display or insufficient time to publicise, may damage your reputation.

After the exhibition

Always thank everyone who has helped, and keep records of attendances, catalogue sales etc. for future reference. If you have received financial assistance, the people who helped you may need to see copies of your accounts.

CHAPTER 17

Party-plan selling and other opportunities

Selling your products directly to the customer is the most profitable option for many craftworkers, but it can be difficult to do if you do not have your own studio where you can retail. Craft fairs are one solution, but these do not always provide sufficient income or convenient venues.

Another option is to take your goods directly to the customer. This type of selling is known as "party plan" because the original parties were held in people's houses, but nowadays parties can be held virtually anywhere: works canteens, village halls, or even a tent in someone's garden.

Party plan

The image of selling by party plan has improved since its first associations with plastic kitchenware. It is now one of the most successful methods of direct marketing, and can be used to good advantage by craftworkers. It has many benefits, including providing a captive audience, occupying a short period of time, having low overheads and requiring less stock than a fair or market. It can also provide customer feedback for craftworkers who usually supply shops and galleries and do not deal directly with the customer.

If you are not skilled at selling, it is possible to find someone to run the parties for you. Remember that the range of products on sale needs to be varied and interesting if it is to keep people entertained for a couple of hours, so you may need to consider combining your work with other craftworkers in order to provide variety.

How to get started

As with any business, you need to plan ahead. Work out the level of commission you can afford, and prepare some printed price lists and order forms.

Where to hold a party

Most people begin by holding a party in their own or a friend's home. Organisations and charities also run parties in halls and other venues. You should aim to book at least one future party at each event to ensure continuity.

What to sell

You need a range of products with good profit margins, as the party will not be profitable if it comprises 20 guests who each buy a £1.99 fridge magnet! This method of selling works particularly well when customers can collect things like sets of pottery.

Incentives

Work out how much you can afford to give the host; it is generally 10-20% of the value of goods sold. Charities will want cash, so you will need to take this into account. Some party planners give everyone a small gift, e.g. a key- ring, and others play a game with a small prize to break the ice.

Finance

Usually, people will spend more if they order on the night and pay later. Ask everyone to fill in an order form – the host will need a copy of these if she is to collect the money.

Arrange the delivery date at the party and arrange for the host to collect the money – do not leave goods unpaid for. If you cannot deliver the item, ring the customer and ask if they will accept an alternative – always keep a note of all customers' names and contact details.

A different slant

The traditional method of holding a party in someone's house and taking orders can be varied to provide a more focused event. For example, Christine Cummings, a ceramicist, joins forces once a year with other craftworkers and holds a Sale Day. They use this as an opportunity to sell "seconds", and they provide refreshments and generally make it an entertaining occasion. Of course, not everyone is fortunate enough to have a farm with a barn at their disposal, but a large garden with a couple of frame tents could be utilised. They promote the event by collecting customers' addresses throughout the year and sending a mailshot inviting people to the sale. Entry is by invitation only. Care needs to be taken that this type of event does not become a craft fair, and you must make sure that you are not infringing planning regulations.

For a successful party, remember:

- Make it entertaining – it is a social occasion.
- Offer incentives for booking future parties.
- Include a re-order form with all orders.
- Keep a list of all customers and add them to your mailing list.
- Avoid school holidays.

Rent-a-Shelf

Some galleries and retail outlets now offer a "rent-a-shelf" scheme. This is useful if you trade mainly online, as it allows you to direct customers to a shop where they can physically see your work. Although sometimes expensive, it can be cost-effective if you are paying out a lot of money for craft fairs, spending a lot of time manning the stand, and not taking much money.

The advantage over supplying a gallery on sale-or-return is that you generally choose which of your work to display, and create your display it yourself, giving you control over how your work looks.

Checklist for a rent-a-shelf scheme

- How many similar makers do they stock?
- Who does the selling – a professional salesperson can make all the difference.
- Do they stock any bought-in goods?
- How often do they pay you?

TOP TIP

give it at least 3 months, preferably longer; and remember to direct your customers to the shop!

CHAPTER 18
Networking

Keeping in touch with other craftworkers and artists is vital. You will benefit from the exchange of ideas and support, and will find reassurance in talking to other people in your situation. Many creatives work in isolation, and unless they make an effort to keep in contact they will miss out on opportunities to market their work, enter for exhibitions, and find out what is going on in their field.

What is a network?

A network is simply a group of people who communicate with each other, support each other and help each other with their work. If you share studio space, or work in a craft centre, there will be a natural exchange of information. But if you work alone, you have to make some effort to maintain contacts, for example by joining a Craft Guild, Association, or Artists Group subscribing to a publication, or using the Internet.

Your immediate network

When you start out, don't forget to make use of your immediate network. Family, friends, colleagues and neighbours can all help you spread the word that you are now in business. Let all these people know when you are visiting your first craft fair or having your first exhibition – hopefully they will all come along, and may even buy something. Remember, you need all the friends you can get to help you get established.

Expanding your contacts

To ensure that you receive current information, make sure that your name is on all the appropriate mailing lists. The Arts Council, arts associations, galleries, local government arts departments, the Crafts Council, and others, all keep lists of craftworkers to whom they regularly send information. If you attend craft fairs, you need to be on the organisers' lists too.

Craft Guilds and Associations

There may be a craft guild in your area; you could ask at your local Arts Council or library. The Crafts Council keeps a list of guilds, and craft-related publications often feature and sometimes list guilds. To find out about the effectiveness of a guild, you need to ask the members. Some guilds exist mainly to promote the craft educationally; others, to provide a market for their members' crafts.

Types of Guilds

Some guilds accept work from all types of craftworker, and it is simply a matter of turning up and asking to join. Others are very strict about membership and will want to see samples of your work. Some guilds only accept one type of craft. Just occasionally, a guild will only admit one member for each craft. This can be disappointing, but if they organise fairs they may want to present a wide range of different crafts, so it's still worth staying in touch.

Before joining a guild

There are over 200 guilds in the UK, so there will probably be one near you that is suitable. Before joining, decide what you want from a guild: do you want an outlet for your product or do you want the status that membership might give you? Check out the benefits of membership, any training offered, how often members meet, fees, etc. You may benefit from belonging both to a local guild with different crafts and to a national guild for your specific craft. This should give you access to the widest range of services.

Guilds rely on their members to perform a lot of functions, so if you want your guild to be a success then be prepared to play your part in helping the organisation.

Artists' networks

There are two main networks for artists:

- a-n, formerly the Artists' Information Network, aims to stimulate and support contemporary visual arts practice from the artist's perspective. They provide insurance and other help for practicing artists. See www.a-n.co.uk
- The Society for All Artists (SAA) supports anyone wanting to develop their artistic streak. Particularly good for those who want to earn part of their income by teaching. www.SAA.co.uk

Small business organisations

If you want to build a more commercial type of business, it may be useful to belong to a small business organisation. Organisations such as the Forum of Private Business and the Federation of Small Businesses provide their members with discounted insurance, free legal helplines, etc.; these can add up to considerable savings. Locally there may be a small business club, which you might find useful. There are also special organisations for women in business and young people in business.

Take advantage of invitations to meetings; take your business cards and talk to as many people as possible. Some people do not find this easy, but it does get easier with practice, and can prove very rewarding for your business.

How to network

Many people confuse networking with socialising, and wander around having a lovely chat and enjoying the event! You are in business now, and you must make maximum use of every opportunity. So try the following approach:

- Talk to as many people as possible. They won't all remember your name, but a smile and "hello, I'm Jane Smith, I make jewellery" is all it needs to start talking. Move around; don't stick with one person, however fascinating.
- If you get stuck with someone, suggest you both go and join another group; this will enable you to move on without leaving them alone.
- Collect as many business cards as possible. Offer yours first and then ask for theirs. Try to jot something about the person on the back, particularly if they showed an interest in your work.
- Set a target before attending an event such as:
    - To find 3 people to send information to
    - To meet one gallery owner
    - To collect 10 business cards.

This will give you a focus and stop you from merely socialising!

TOP TIP
Wherever you meet people, you have a networking opportunity, whether it's the school gates or the queue in the supermarket. Always have your business cards or postcards ready to hand out.

Part 4

Marketing

CHAPTER 19

A marketing plan

Everyone learns about the importance of having a business plan, but few remember that a marketing plan is just as important, if not more so. If you don't plan how to sell your work, the chances are you won't sell any.

Very rarely do people buy something at first glance. They follow a process that marketers call **AIDA:**

Attention
Interest
Desire
Action

In other words, you first have to gain their attention, then their interest, then you need them to want your products, and finally you need to enable them to take action. So the beginning of your marketing plan could be to write down how you plan to make each of these steps happen.

Creating a marketing plan

Writing a marketing plan is a useful exercise both when you start selling, and if you find sales are slowing and you are not sure why. Writing a plan can help you identify how you can improve the situation. Simply answer the following questions and you will have the basis of a plan.

Your business and your customers

What are you trying to achieve? Do you want to earn a living, are you just trying to make some extra income, or do you want to see your work in John Lewis? Everyone has a goal – what's yours?

Why will people buy your products? Are they gifts, household items, decorative, fashionable? Why is your work desirable, compared to the work of one of your competitors? Do people think it will increase in value? If you understand why people buy your products it will make it easier to market them.

Who are you trying to sell to? If you are selling recycled, eco-friendly products, you might be best suited to a craft fair next to a farmers' market. If your products are luxury items, you might need a gallery in an upmarket location. Think about where your customers shop; but also, what they value. Then you can tailor the way you present your work so it appeals to them, and emphasise the things about it that they will feel are important.

Your identity

What is the name of your business? Many makers use their own names, and this is fine unless you hope to build up a large business and sell it, when you would also have to sell your name. Avoid fancy names that confuse people. Artists will need to use their own name, but if another artist already uses it, consider using your middle name or a nickname.

Do you have/need a strapline? A strapline is a very short description of your work. If you are trading under the name Sue Smith, you might use the strapline "contemporary silver jewellery" to ensure people know what your product is.

Do you have/need a logo? Most professional makers say that the only images on your stationery or adverts should be of your work.

Have you registered your domain name? Although you can start selling your work without a website, it is a good idea to register your domain name as soon as possible. Your own name might not be available so you might have to add another word or use a hyphen, e.g. www.susan- smith-jewellery.

co.uk. It is cheap to register a domain name: just Google "domain names" for a range of companies that can help.

Your budget

Every business owner has an amount they want to spend on marketing. Decide on what this is for you, and plan accordingly. This prevents you from being persuaded to spend money on advertising, which won't work for you.

Creating a plan

Once you have all this information, set some SMART goals. Everyone has goals they want to achieve, but in order to make them achievable they need to be

SMART:

Specific

Measurable

Attainable

Relevant

Timed.

Examples of SMART goals:

To book 3 stalls at craft fairs by the end of the month.

To find 4 galleries to stock my work by the end of the year.

To have my work featured in one major magazine this year.

To enter 2 exhibitions this year.

Write your goals down

The following chapters in this section will give you information and ideas about different strands of marketing activity that will help you to achieve your goals – so read them, decide which ones you want to put into practice, and add the details of what actions you will take, and when, to your plan.

CHAPTER 20
Market research

C arrying out some market research will help you find out if you have a potential customer, and can save you from wasting a lot of time making things that will not sell. It's not difficult to do: you can carry out basic market research on a new product at a craft fair, or by creating an online survey on Facebook and emailing your existing customers a link to it, or by getting together a focus group. Market research can also stimulate new ideas: by listening to what people say, you might find an idea for a new product or a way to make your existing products more saleable.

Being market-ready
There is no point marketing a product that is not market-ready. Don't start marketing your work before you can answer, "yes" to the following:

- Is your work of sufficient quality for people to purchase it?
- Are you working in a style that people want?
- Do you have enough work ready to sell?
- Are you able to produce enough pieces for potential buyers?
- Is your product free of any legal constraints or problems that might limit you in bringing it to market?

How to conduct market research

When researching a new product or business idea, evaluate it by:

- using your own experience – do you have experience of selling or buying similar work?
- finding independent views – ask other people's opinions, perhaps using a questionnaire at a fair, or online using a tool such as Survey Monkey.
- collecting information on the sector – find out which colours are fashionable, read interior design blogs or fashion websites and magazines.
- networking – gather information informally from friends and colleagues at networking events.

Here are some of the types of research that you might find useful:

Profiling your customers

When marketing your work, you need to have a clear picture in mind of the sort of person who will buy it. Constructing a profile of a typical customer is a useful exercise. Try to imagine the type of person who would be interested in buying your work, and answer the following questions:

- What is their age?
- Are they male or female?
- Where do they live?
- What is their level of income?
- What type of job do they have?
- Why will they be buying your goods?
- What are their leisure activities?
- What do they read?
- Where do they shop – department stores, craft fairs, tourist shops, galleries?

Test marketing

If you are just starting out, you need to test whether there is a market for your work.

- Take a stand at a craft fair, art fair or farmers' market; anywhere where you think your potential customers (see your customer profile) might shop
- Exhibit some work on an Internet site, which allows people to sell work
- Hold a focus group - get together a group of people (preferably not all friends) and display your work. Give them an anonymous questionnaire to comment on your work and say whether they would buy it and how much they would pay.

Competitors

Although you might not like the idea, you will have competitors. You need to know who they are, how they sell their work and how much they charge.

- Name three of your competitors.
- List three of their strengths and three of their weaknesses.
- List two places they sell their work.
- What are their price points?

Consider this information carefully. Has it affected your plans?
Using your research

The more you understand your customers, the easier it will be to reach them and the more successful your business. For instance:

- If you are targeting the collectors' market, you need to visit fairs that collectors visit. These are likely to be specialist fairs such as Potfest rather then a local craft fair.
- If your customers do their shopping online, you need to make sure you have a strong Internet presence.
- Could you use the words you have identified as key words in your Internet marketing to attract new customers?

Using negative feedback

Carrying out market research can have a positive effect when everyone loves your products. However sometimes you obtain a negative response. If you take this information and use your creative skills to solve the problem before you start producing in quantity, you can save yourself a lot of money.

For example:

- Stacey's soft toy rabbits were very popular with focus groups, except that people felt they were expensive. She solved the problem by making them smaller, and therefore cheaper.
- John's paintings were popular but they were in wooden frames, and everyone preferred silver. A change of frame increased his sales.

CHAPTER 21
Creating a brand and reputation

As a creative, your image and that of your business will always be intertwined. Every time you come into contact with your customers, you send them messages about you and your business. This evolves into a brand when people start to recognise and remember the message you are sending, and to think of your brand name or company name as an assurance of what they will get from you.

Brand image is the strongest factor influencing a customer's perceptions of your business. It reflects the quality of your products, your level of efficiency, your style, and your values. A positive brand image can be the difference between failure and success.

As an artist your reputation is really important. Although you may not think of yourself as a "brand", similar principles apply. Artists who focus on a certain type of work often find it easier to get a following: collectors particularly like work that is recognisable by a particular artist. This doesn't stop you trying new work, but it may mean you are building a different "brand".

What is a brand image?

Every time you contact your customers, you are influencing the way they think about you. Whether it's at a craft fair or over the telephone, subconsciously people will give you a character, and this often determines why someone buys one person's work rather than another's. Customers will prefer certain businesses because they are made to feel important.

Many craftworkers consider that their image is simply the look of their stationery, and look no further than the printed word. This is a mistake; your image should run through your whole business. Because a craft business is very personal and reflects the image of the craftworker, your personal image and even your appearance is important. For an artist it will include the way your work is framed and the subject matter.

Creating an image

Obtaining the right image need not be expensive but it does require a lot of thought, particularly in the initial stages. If you employ professionals such as graphic designers, they should insist on meeting you and talking to you about your image of the business and the type of customers you intend to serve. Be very wary of printers who have an artist available, as they may just feed you a logo off a computer package and you could find you are using the same logo as a number of other companies. If you require a logo and cannot afford to employ a graphic designer, you might find an art student willing to supply a few samples for a modest fee or a fellow craftworker with these skills.

Which image?

There are two crucial factors in deciding the type of image to aim for with your business. The first is your own personality, and the second is the market you are aiming for.

Your personality

Creative businesses almost inevitably project the image of their owner. This is particularly true if you have a lot of personal contact with your customers and if you have a strong character. For this reason it is important that the image of the business reflects your personality. It is a lot easier to build on your own characteristics rather than trying to invent a personality that doesn't suit you. Compare successful entrepreneurs and their companies: Richard Branson and Virgin, Emma Bridgewater and Cath Kidston are obvious examples, but consider the small business people that you know. How many of them really fit their businesses, and are they the successful ones?

Your market

The image of a business aiming at the top end of the gallery market will be entirely different from that of a business trading mainly through local craft fairs. Both businesses may well be extremely profitable, but for different reasons. It is essential when planning your image that you know which market you are aiming at. It often helps to have a visual image of your customer – look back at Chapter 13 for some ideas on how to do this.

The name of the business

If you are just starting a business, consider the name very carefully. A trading name that reflects exactly the required image can be an enormous advantage. It should be easy to remember and should trip off the tongue easily. Options include

- using your own name e.g. Jane Birch
- using the name of a local town, river or county, e.g. Avon Crafts
- using a descriptive name, e.g. Ceramic Cats
- using something catchy, e.g. Two's Company

If you have trouble deciding on a name, have a brainstorming session. Write down all the names you can think of, and use a thesaurus to list associated words. Choose five or six possibilities and check online, and with a craftworkers' directory, that there isn't another business with a similar name. Ask your friends to consider the remaining titles and the image they project. If you are planning to sell abroad, make sure the words don't mean something inappropriate in another language. Choose a name that's easy to remember and spell, so people will be able to find your website easily.

House colours

Choice of colour for your publicity material is very important, as colours trigger people's perceptions. Every colour portrays a different image.

- Dark colours tend to be smart and traditional: deep green, burgundy and navy blue are often used by up-market retailers to suggest quality.
- Yellows are cheerful and fun, and can be introduced as a second colour to promote a more modern image.
- Red is the best-selling colour, but some shades can convey cheapness.
- Green and brown give a rustic homespun impression. Brown used alone can be very dull; put gold with dark green for an upmarket image.
- Mid-tone greens are good for interiors and environmental products.
- Pastel shades are generally considered feminine and unbusinesslike but can therefore be ideal for some types of product, such as lingerie.

If you intend to export, check that the colours you choose do not convey any adverse message in the country you plan to sell in. For instance, white is associated with death in Japan.

Lettering style

Find a typeface that suits your work and fits in with the rest of your image, and use it throughout your publicity – letterheads, website, leaflets, brochure. Make sure the style you choose is easily readable and not fancy – and also that it's a commonly available or free font. Desktop publishing computer programs make it easier to produce documents professionally. Many colleges offer desktop publishing courses, which can save you a fortune.

You

Although no-one expects a craftworker to sell at a craft fair wearing a formal suit, or an artist to attend a Preview in a tuxedo it is important to wear the right clothes for the right occasions. Only very successful artists and craftworkers can afford to be bohemian. Be neat and tidy at all times; wear more formal clothes for the interview with the bank manager; and when selling, wear your own goods if appropriate. T-shirts featuring your own artwork can prove both a good advertisement and a good seller.

The artist's statement

Every artist should have an artist's statement in his or her portfolio. It should be available on your website, and printed out and used at exhibitions.

An artist's statement is a short piece of text written by you, the creative mind behind it all, to accompany a particular painting or group of paintings. You should take time writing your statement; it is a vital selling tool, promoting and explaining your work to potential buyers, exhibition curators, critics, fellow artists, and casual browsers.

At its best, an artist's statement reads easily, is informative, and adds to the reader's understanding of the artist and the painting. At its worst, an artist's statement is difficult to understand or rambles on, is pretentious, and irritates rather than informs (or even provokes laughter).

How long should an artist's statement be?

It is a good idea to have two versions of the statement: a shorter version to put on your website and use as a handout at exhibitions, and a longer statement to give to curators etc. Aim at around 100 words, or three short paragraphs, for the shorter version.

What should an artist's statement say?

An artist's statement should be an explanation of your painting style and your subjects or themes. Add a bit about your approach or philosophy if you wish: what influences you when your decide what to paint. Mention your education if appropriate, specifically if you've studied art. (The closer you are to the date you left Art College, the more relevant this is).

If there are artists (living or dead) who have influenced or inspired you, name them, and state what it is about them that inspires you. Mention any significant awards you have won, exhibitions you have participated in, collections your paintings appear in or significant sales you have made, and art organisations or societies you belong to,

Remember, though, you're aiming to create professional credibility by highlighting your achievements, not providing a full CV. If you don't have a formal art qualification, don't worry – it's your paintings that make you an artist, not your qualifications.

TOP TIP
update your statement for every exhibition. Your body of work will be changing and growing, and this should be reflected in your statement.

CHAPTER 22

Promoting your work

To promote your work successfully, you need to know the following:

• Who you are?

People are always interested in the person behind the work. It's very difficult to build a successful creative business if you are not prepared for people to know about you.

• Why do you make your items?

The story behind your products can attract customers because it makes what they're buying special — and by extension, it makes them feel special. When you produce new items, always tell customers the reason, and the story behind them.

• How is your product different?

What is your USP (Unique Selling Point or Proposition)? Obviously everything you make will be unique, but think about what you offer from your customers' perspective: what is unique about you that can serve their needs? See Chapter 2 for details of how to identify your USP.

- ## Which words would you use to describe your items?

So you are a jeweller. You make jewellery – and so do lots of other people. What adjectives can you use to differentiate yourself from your competition and position yourself in the market? Try the 20-10-4 exercise: choose 20 words to describe your brand, then whittle them down to 10, then 4. The jeweller whose four words are "silver, elegant, contemporary and exclusive" appeals in a different way to the customer than one whose words are "funky, recycled, colourful and trendy."

- ## Who are your customers?

Don't fall into the trap of trying to be everything to everybody. Think about who your likely customers might be, and build a brand to appeal to them. How old are they, what kinds of TV shows do they like, how much money do they make, where do they live – anything that might help you zero in on prospective buyers' mindsets.

Building your brand/reputation

When you have answered the above questions, you have the beginnings of your brand or "story". Now you need to tell this story to your customers. Before you start to advertise and promote your work you need to make it as secure as possible and prevent people from copying it.

Registering a trademark

Trademarks are signs, symbols, logos, words, sounds or music (such as jingles) that distinguish your products and services from those of your competitors. A trademark can be one of the most powerful marketing tools you have, and can help people recognise the quality and design of your product.

A trademark must be distinctive for the goods and services you use it for. Providing you can represent your trademark in words and pictures, you can register it in the UK. Registering it establishes in law that it is your trademark and belongs to you alone. You then have an automatic right to sue anybody who infringes it. In fact just registering it can serve as a deterrent to people who might otherwise infringe it.

To register a trademark, you need to apply to the UK Intellectual Property Office (UK-IPO). The forms and details of the fees payable are on their website www.uk-ipo.com.

To register your business, go to www.start.biz

Ways to advertise and promote your business

Not all these methods will suit your business, but the list is included because most people only use business cards, fliers, brochures or Facebook. Try something different, using your own designs where possible.

Places to Advertise

Mailshots	Buses
Fliers	Newspapers
Sports grounds	Hoardings
Directories	Car Park Tickets
Yellow Pages	Brochures
Thomson	Carrier Bags
Local Yell.com	Catalogues
Magazines	Cinema
Shop windows	Posters
Vehicles	Trade Journals
Notice Boards	Labels
Business Cards	Postcards
Magazines	Emails

Promotional items

Baseball caps	Loyalty Cards
Beer mats	Mugs and Glasses
Calendars	Badges

Christmas cards

Mouse mats

USB sticks

Coupons/vouchers

Diaries

Uniforms

Notebooks

Pens

T-shirts

Umbrellas

Balloons

Promotional ideas

Celebrities

Charity events

Questionnaires

Giving talks

Trade fairs

Sponsorship

Networking

Competitions

Fairs/Exhibitions

Golf Days

Media

Website

Electronic billboards

Radio

MySpace

YouTube

Blogs

Google Ad words

Viral Marketing

Television

Social Networking

Text Messages

Point of Sale

Show Cards

Samples

TOP TIP

Don't forget that word of mouth is your best advertisement and make sure that your customer services encourages people to recommend you to their friends.

Producing a brochure

A brochure can be a very useful marketing tool. It can either be printed, or on your website, or both. The brochure doesn't need to be very elaborate if you do not have the funding; low-cost Internet printers will print small quantities for you, and you can design it yourself to save costs. Having good colour photographs is really important. The content of the brochure can vary, but here are some suggestions:

Your brochure should include:
Name of your business
Your address, phone number, web address, Twitter, Facebook, etc.
Photos of your work
Descriptive text about the pieces shown
List of shows you attend
Awards you have won
Your artistic philosophy or artist's statement
Testimonials/quotes

You should think about:
Cover design
What is going on the back page
Typeface/font
Layout: limit the amount of text, and don't over-design.
Colour, type and weight of paper
Quantity: how many will you have printed?
Can you store them?
Inserts: do you need an insert that can be regularly updated, e.g. a price list?

As a general rule, printed brochures should:

- contain no more than four A5 pages
- be written in simple English, avoiding technical jargon
- be illustrated
- not contain prices. These should be on a separate sheet if they need to be included, as they will date quickly.

CHAPTER 23

Advertising

Most people think of advertising as putting an advert in the newspaper. This chapter is aimed at helping you create adverts of all kinds, whether they are postcards for an exhibition, promotions on the Internet or a brochure advertising your workshops.

Many creatives do not feel comfortable with advertising, perhaps due to unhappy experiences or the fact that it is difficult to monitor the results. The industrialist Lord Leverhulme is quoted as having said, "Half the money I spend on advertising is wasted. My problem is to find out which half".

Why advertise?

The advantage of advertising over other forms of promotion such as public relations is that you have direct control over exactly what is published and when. This can be very important, particularly if you are launching a new product or opening a studio and want to link various types of promotion. Reckless spending on advertising is foolish. What is needed is a properly thought-out campaign with definite objectives.

To be successful, an advertising campaign requires a series of carefully planned advertisements, which are part of an overall promotional scheme.

To succeed with advertising you need to know:

- Why are you advertising?
- Who are you targeting?
- Where do you intend to advertise?
- When do you want to advertise?

Reasons for advertising might be:

- to attract new buyers
- to announce a new product
- to highlight a promotion
- to attract stockists
- to educate and/or inform
- to build customer loyalty and brand recognition
- to instill confidence in a product

How much should I spend?

Deciding the size of your advertising budget is difficult. A new studio may need to spend heavily to establish a presence in the market, but a more established one may only need to reinforce its position. Experience is the best guide; or look at how much your competitors are spending.

Your advertising budget is part of your promotional budget, which will also include exhibitions and special events. Decide how much you intend to spend over the next year and stick to your budget. Do not be tempted to cut back if sales improve, although if one advert is performing better than the others it may be worth re-allocating resources.

Time, not money

There are ways to advertise and promote your work, which take time rather than money. These include social media, sending press releases, and using your website. Remember that your time is worth money, so although it may appear free, in fact it has a cost.

How to write an advertisement

When you write an advertisement, always try to focus on your customer. What do they need to know? Remember you will only have a few seconds to make an impact. Good advertisements follow the **AIDA** formula:

- **A**ttention – can be aroused by a headline and/or picture
- **I**nterest – copy must be of interest
- **D**esire – seeks to persuade the customer
- **A**ction – something extra to spur the customer on to buying e.g. a coupon, trial offer, etc.

Use a professional approach and draw up a "creative brief" for your advertisement. The main points to cover in a creative brief are:

- the objectives – what do you want to achieve?
- the target audience – who are your customers?
- the USP (Unique Selling Point) – what is the main benefit of the product?
- the supporting evidence – facts and figures.

To create advertising copy, write down the answers to the following questions:

- How is the object made?
- What does it do?

- What does it look like?
- Does it save money?
- Is it valuable?
- Is it fashionable?
- Does it offer good value for money?
- Is it collectable?

Where to advertise

- Local paper – if you want to attract people to your studio
- Craft fair brochure – to ensure customers visit your stand
- Craft magazine – for new stockists
- Interiors magazines – for direct sales
- County magazines – for upmarket customers
- The Internet – there are numerous opportunities to advertise online, some free, and some expensive; but follow the rules above for maximum impact.

TOP TIP
when you put items on social media about your business you are effectively advertising and should follow the guidelines above.

CHAPTER 24

Public Relations

What is PR?

Few people understand the nature and value of public relations. It is often seen as "free advertising", but in fact it is about helping you create a positive image in the press while keeping your customers informed about what is happening with your business. As it is an extremely cost-effective method of influencing people, you should use it as widely as possible. If you win an award, are exhibiting at an unusual venue, or produce a new product, then PR can help you tell your customers about it.

PR can help an artist to acquire and retain a good reputation. It can also improve the image of the business, and can be useful in countering any negative publicity. Small businesses often dismiss PR as being irrelevant to their needs, but all businesses have a "public". Your public could include your suppliers, your creditors, authorities, the general public, customers and potential customers. A glance at your local newspaper or trade press will show which makers are adept at PR. Are you losing out to your rivals who are using PR?

There is no magic to PR; any creative can practice it. You can teach yourself how to use PR to your advantage; in fact you may already be using some of the techniques without being aware of it. PR is simply about building a relationship with the media, learning to write a press release, and promoting your business in the media at every opportunity.

Measuring the benefits of PR is difficult, but after a well-planned PR campaign it should be possible to see the benefits in increased market share, customer loyalty, and in a general increased awareness of your products.

The press release

One of the easiest and most effective methods of contacting the media is with a press release. This is a written statement from you containing all the details about the promotion. A press release should be attractive and readily usable by reporters. It should, as far as possible, be written in the style of the publication; for example, a press release for a trade journal may contain technical data, which would be of little interest to a local paper.

The main ingredients of a press release are:

- The headline – this should give some indication of the content. There is no need to try and think of some clever phrase, as most reporters prefer to write their own headlines when filing a story.
- The beginning – as with a good book, the first line is very important and needs to catch the reader's attention straight away.
- The facts – a press release should contain the five 'W's: Who, What, Where, When and Why.
- Quotes – always try to give the story a personal angle. A quote from a satisfied customer is useful, as is a photograph of the people involved.
- Contact details – make sure you include details of how an interested reporter can contact you, and links to your website etc. for further information.

The advantages of using a press release are:

- Because it is in writing, you have control of its contents.
- You have a permanent record.

- You are not pressured by an over-zealous reporter.
- You control the timing of the press release. (However, not all journalists' honour embargo dates, so if it is very sensitive, send it out after the event.)
- It is very cost-effective.
  Having decided to send a press release, you must remember that editors receive thousands of press releases every month, and for yours to be used requires that it should have two extra things:
- It should be written in journalistic style – see the text box on rules for writing a press release.
- It should be newsworthy. Find an interesting angle and it is more likely your information will be used.

Rules for writing a press release

- **Use eye-catching paper, something that attracts attention without detracting from the message.**
- **Use simple words and short sentences.**
- **Avoid jargon and acronyms, unless writing for the trade press.**
- **Make sure all trade and technical terms and descriptions are correct.**
- **Keep it as short as possible. One side of A4, with an extra page of background if necessary, is ideal.**
- **Write only on one side of the paper.**
- **Use wide margins, double spacing and a clear typeface.**
- **Finish the release with the words ENDS followed by a contact name and number.**
- **Choose a positive headline.**
- **Answer the 5 'W's, preferably in the first paragraph.**
- **Write news, not views.**
- **Always double-check spelling of names etc.**
- **Always date the release. If not for immediate publication, state the embargo date.**

- **Include a good quote if possible.**
- **Include a good photograph if possible; clearly label it and identify all the subjects in it.**
- **Send it to the right person. A telephone call or a look at the paper's website will tell you who.**
- **Keep a copy of everything you send.**

Where to send your press release

To maximise the effect of your promotion, you need to send press releases to the most appropriate media. The variety of publications and broadcasting media is huge, and they have a great appetite for news. In choosing the right media you need to consider their needs and customers as well as your own.

Newsagents, even the major ones, carry only a fraction of the journals available. To find out the names of publications and their address, consult a copy of www.bradinsight.com, a subscription-based online directory which lists every newspaper, business journal, consumer publication, independent TV and commercial radio station in the U.K. It's worth checking at your local library if they have access. Alternatively, www.magazinesubscriptions.co.uk has a fairly comprehensive list of publications.

You could send your press release to:

- **Local newspapers** – This is probably the best place to start, as they are always looking for local news with human interest. The installation of a new machine will not usually merit much attention but selling your ceramic tiles to a Hollywood star would be (yes, it has happened to a Manchester maker!)
- **Trade press** – There are a wide variety of newspapers and magazines, which rarely appear on newsagents' shelves. These are often distributed free or under subscription to members of a particular trade. These publications rely on press releases to keep them up to date with developments. Read them carefully and decide which

section your press release will fit into: new products, appointments, exhibitions, etc. Their deadline for copy will probably be earlier than the local press, so make sure that you send the information in time for publication.

- **Consumer magazines** – These do not generally contain many news items. Their deadline date for editorial is usually two months before production. Contacting the advertising department for a list of future features could lead you to find a connection with your product. Some of these magazines will give you editorial space if you advertise, and it is always worth trying to negotiate this if their customers are particularly important to you. If you can, make contact with the editorial staff.

- **National/regional newspapers** – To stand any chance of being mentioned in national or regional newspapers, your story will need to have a wider appeal. Any connection with a current news story is obviously a help. With such a wide circulation, any mention of your promotion will be valuable. Many local reporters feed stories to the regional and national press, so you may find your story appearing in other publications via this method.

- **Local radio** – This attracts the same sort of audience as local newspapers, and can be a very effective medium. However, before approaching radio, you need to have someone prepared and able to be interviewed. If the station is running a promotion you might be able to link to it, e.g. Small Business Week or Job Week. They also often cover local events, so if you are sponsoring one, don't forget invite them – they may even broadcast from there if the event is interesting enough.

- **Television** – To attract television attention your story will need to have a strong visual content. Regional news programmes will often cover stories concerning celebrities or dramatic events if given sufficient notice. You should never rely on television coverage in case a major news story breaks on the day you were due to appear and you end up on the cutting-room floor. If you really want television coverage, try to schedule your promotion for the quiet times: the first week in January or during the summer holidays. Avoid clashing with national promotions such as Children in Need. Do not dismiss television as being too grand – it is a very persuasive medium and even the smallest mention can be very effective.

- **Online** – You can also post your story to websites, which are relevant to your business.

Contacting the press

One advantage of PR is that people tend to believe what they read in an article or news item more than they do an advertisement. You will also reach people you wouldn't normally target, and this can be very positive for a growing company.

When talking to a journalist, always assume that anything you say will appear in print. You need to know the journalist very well before you can talk "off the record". Prepared statements best handle sensitive issues, and it can be a good idea to practice writing these before a crisis actually occurs.

Worry about being misreported and losing control of a campaign is natural, but your confidence to work with the press will grow as you become more experienced. Initially you will probably be dealing with local newspapers and radio and the trade press, not the national dailies, who are looking for the more "exciting" type of story.

Some publications have a reputation for misquoting people and treating them badly – try to avoid contact with them, particularly if your business is suffering from the type of problems, which appeal to this type of publication. The best action is to say nothing, and if the situation demands it, contact a solicitor to speak on your behalf.

Some publications will only accept editorial from advertisers: this can work to your advantage and disadvantage. If you would consider advertising in the publication anyway then it is probably worth negotiating a deal; otherwise, decline politely.

If you are to persuade a journalist to print your story, you will need an "angle", something that makes your product or company newsworthy. No matter how good your relationship is, no journalist is going to risk their reputation by publishing dull and uninteresting news.

Always remember when dealing with the press:

- Don't attempt to mislead the media with false claims
- Don't expect preferential treatment if you advertise. They have a product to sell too, and will use the best material available.
- Don't expect editors to be as excited as you are about your promotion
- Don't leave everything to the last minute and then expect action.
- Don't over-promote the name of your company or product.
- Don't forget to thank them if they use your release.
- Don't try to bribe the journalist.

What to promote

You may have decided that PR seems like a good idea but cannot think of anything about your business that could be promoted. Consider what makes a good story:

- Relevance to the media's readership/customers
- Human interest
- Topicality
- Timing
- Entertainment value, originality or humour
- Availability of good photos

So what can you offer? Have you recently changed your product? Is it a new development? Have you changed name so you can sell abroad? Have you won an award? Are you taking part in a special event or promo□on? Why not sponsor an event or do something for charity?

Whatever you do, tell the press about it – you never know what publicity it might bring you.

See the following page for a sample press release.

TOP TIP
Don't forget to include the media on the internet when conducting a campaign.

Littleborough Craft Guild

8 Church Street, Littleborough, Lancashire OL15 9AB Tel 01706 33333
www.littleboroughcraftguild.com

PRESS RELEASE

15th November 2015

Unique gifts for Christmas

Littleborough Craft Guild will be holding their 5th Annual Christmas Gift Fair from 7-14th December 2015 at the Civic Hall.

Over 20 craftworkers will be exhibiting, including wood turner Geoff Hallworth, textile artist Diane Ainsworth, jeweller Judith Hemingway and ceramicist Stuart Daniels. Local celebrity Susan Samson will be exhibiting her recycled gifts, which she recently demonstrated on ITV's This Morning. She won the New Business Award at the British Craft Fair in York this year and exhibits widely all over the country.

The exhibition, which is a selling exhibition, is always very popular and customers are advised to come early to have the widest choice.

Elizabeth Watson, Guild Chairman, said, 'Our Christmas exhibitions are always popular as people look for something different to give as presents. The opening of the Pennine Canal is attracting more tourists to the area so we expect to increase the number of visitors from last year's record.'

The Civic Hall is situated on Church Street and has FREE parking outside. It is open every day during the exhibition from 10-5 p.m. Refreshments are available.

Littleborough is accessible by train from Manchester and Leeds and is approximately 10 minutes from J21 of the M62.

Ends

For further information contact Elizabeth Watson Tel. 07801 444444
Email Lizwatson@hotmail.com
Image attached

Part 5

Using the Internet

CHAPTER 25

Your web presence

I t's virtually impossible to run any type of business without access to a computer. Most people now use computers on a regular basis. If you find it difficult to use one, it is strongly recommended that you get help to learn. Many areas still have free classes: ask at your local library or local college. You can run a business without a computer, but you will run a better business with one. If you have struggled with a computer you might find a table easier to use.

In a world where the Internet is part of daily life, everyone trying to sell their work should have a web presence. This does not need to be a website: many successful craft businesses have been run from a blog.

Do you need a website?

If you want to sell your work online you have two choices: set up your own website, or sell via other people's websites. There are a lot of websites where you can show your work, and some of them are really effective. The advantage of using a selling site is that they will have larger resources to drive traffic to your page. The disadvantage is that you will be alongside your competitors. You may decide to have your own website to promote your work, and then sell your work over selling sites.

Websites do three main things: you might want your website to do all three, or just one.

Provide information

If all you want your website to do is point people in your direction, then a simple one-page site with your name and contact details is sufficient. But this won't highlight your products or tell people about you.

Build your reputation

In order to build a reputation, so people start to recognise your work and know who you are, you need a website that contains information about you and your products.

Allow you to sell your work

If you want to sell online, you will need an e-commerce site. This can be simple (people select goods and pay through PayPal) or more complex, with a brochure, a basket and options to pay on the site.

Domain names

Every website needs a domain name. To choose your name and register it, type "domain names" into Google and you will come up with a variety of options. Go to one of the sites and type in the name you want, to see if it is available. For a business based in the UK, the domain name should end with .co.uk; or if you want to appear international, it should end in .com If you are starting a social enterprise then .org.uk would be an option. Not all names are available, so you may have to add another word to your name e.g. JaneSmithceramics.co.uk or use hyphens, jane-smith.co.uk.

Attracting visitors to your site

A successful website needs visitors. In addition to attracting people via the web, you need to make sure you are building your customer base by other means, such as craft fairs etc. Collect email addresses everywhere you go so you can link people to your site, Facebook account, etc.

Attracting visitors to your site takes time and imagination. Consider some of the following methods to attract more traffic to your site:

- Have a content-rich site that will educate your visitors with information that is relevant and specific to your business.
- Keep your site fresh and current by regularly updating it with articles, news and other information relevant to your target audience.
- Promote your website offline on letterheads, business cards and advertising, so people who find your business in other ways are aware that you have a business website.
- Give visitors a 'call to action' on your site to encourage them to take the next step - for example, "Click here to order" or "Sign up here for our newsletter".
- Include information about your business, such as your postal address and phone number, to show that you have a real, bricks-and-mortar presence and to give visitors an easy way to contact you.

Fresh content

You should update your web content often, to give people a reason to keep coming back. You could include:

- News stories, articles and blog posts. Information about fairs or where your work is on sale is especially important.
- Links to other websites, particularly galleries or shops stocking your work.
- Images and videos, such as photographs of your products. A video of you making your work can be a real draw.
- If you use social media (see Chapter 28 for more information about this), then displaying your Twitter feed or key Facebook posts on your homepage is one way of offering fresh, frequently-updated content, as well as linking different aspects of your web presence.

TOP TIP

Set a time aside regularly, say once a week, to update your website; otherwise you'll either spend too much time on it or ignore it completely.

Search engine optimisation (SEO)

When someone uses a search engine, they type in one or more words describing what they are looking for, such as "designer jewellery Manchester" or "wood turning classes". These words or phrases are known as keywords. The search engine then comes back with a list of web pages, with content that relates to the keywords they typed.

You want to ensure that when customers search for keywords relevant to your business, your website appears as early as possible in the list of results. That is what search engine optimisation (SEO) is all about

The design of your site is an important aspect of achieving a good ranking in search engines, which means people will find your site more easily. Many basic search engine optmisation (SEO) techniques are simple to learn and free to implement.

Get your keywords right. The more carefully you write the textual content of your site and include keywords relevant to your business, the more opportunites there will be for search engine 'spiders' to find it. You can check your level of key wording against other sites using sites such as goRank (see http://tools.seobook.com)

Links

Work on your link popularity. The more websites that link to yours, the higher your site will appear in search results. Try contacting non-competing, related businesses and persuade them to put a link to your website on their site, in return for you doing the same for them.

TOP TIP

Ask someone else to test your site, to see if they find it easy to navigate. You probably know your own site's architecture too well to be sure whether the navigation is intuitive.

CHAPTER 26

Your website

Checklist for a website

Before you begin, you should consider the following practical questions:

- **How will your website be designed and built?** Do you have the skills to build it yourself using an off-the-shelf package, or will you need to commission a web designer?
- **What will your domain name be?** To operate a website you need a registered domain name – this will become the web address of your site. Domain names can be registered online, and there are many businesses offering this service, although their prices vary quite markedly. You can check for the availability of your preferred domain name at Nominet (www.nominet.org.uk). Once registered, you need to renew your domain name regularly (usually every two years) to continue ownership of it.
- **Where will your website be hosted?** A website needs to be hosted on a server with access to the Internet. Small firms usually rely on an outside business to host their websites. They buy a certain amount of space on a web server, and have access to upload and change their

website content as required. There are many companies to choose from who offer this service, and prices vary quite widely. Remember that some cheaper hosting packages might not support things that you want to use, such as ecommerce; might limit the type and size of file you can upload; and might add unwanted advertising to your site. Check the details of your package before you buy. If you do not feel comfortable arranging your own web hosting, a web designer may do this for you, or may advise you.

- **How will you maintain your website?** Do you have the time and technical knowledge to alter your web content when aspects of your business change, and to keep it looking fresh and up-to-date? The degree of skill you need to do this will vary according to how your site is built: if your web designer provides you with a CMS (content management system), it will require little or no technical skill to update.

TOP TIP

Be careful who you use to host your website. It's not uncommon for small web-hosting companies to disappear, leaving you with a website you cannot access.

What are your options for building a website?

- **Doing it yourself using off-the-shelf templates**

This is a very good option: it is relatively simple, cost-effective, and cheap. Using an off-the-shelf website builder, or a set of free website template pages, is one of the simplest ways of setting up a basic site. In most cases, anyone with a basic knowledge of the Internet can set up a website in this way. WordPress is the most popular platform; but many of the companies who register domain names, such as Daily and 123, also offer this service. Vistaprint also offers a website builder service. But if you want complex functionality, or an unusual layout, you might not be able to get this from an off-the-shelf package. Also, be aware that some proprietary site-builders from hosting companies only work with that company's web-servers – so if you ever want to move to a different host, you'll have to rebuild your site from scratch.

- **Hiring a professional web designer**

You may decide to commission a web designer, who will look at your business requirements and determine how the website will fit into your wider strategy. Such an approach is more expensive, but can give your site exactly the look and functionality you seek, and ensure it fits your business objectives.

Designers usually charge by the hour or offer package deals. Charges are likely to range from a few hundred pounds for a simple site to several thousand pounds for a more complex one. You should set out clearly what you want to achieve with your website, and try to get quotes from at least three designers. If you find a website you like, find out who designed it.

Many designers today work in Drupal, WordPress, Joomla and similar – these are tools that you could use yourself, but a designer can customise the available templates and make it look exactly how you want. These platforms also give you a content management system that you can use to update your site easily.

Top Tip

make sure your website looks just as good and is as easy to access on a phone or tablet as the computer.

Developing a project plan for your website

Before you get started on either building your website yourself or commissioning a web designer, you need to develop a brief. Consider:

- What do you want the website for?
- How do you want your customers to contact you via the website?
- What information do you want to include on your website?

You will have to write the text on the website, and usually produce the photographs: a designer will not know enough about your business to do this. Try creating a visual mood board to help the designer work with your vision.

The structure of your site

All websites have a homepage – this is the first page that people see when they type in your web address, and for a very simple site it might be the only page. But when briefing a web designer, they will usually want to know how many other pages you want your site to have. Common things to include are below - remember, you don't have to include all of them!

- A "contact" page, which has all the contact details of your business, and ideally a map to help people find you.
- An "About Me" page, which includes information about you as a creative – your background and training, your artistic philosophy.
- Different strands of your work – if you teach in schools, or run workshops, put information about this on its own page. If you've exhibited a lot, give your exhibitions a page of their own; and if you do a lot of commissioned work, put your commissions on a separate page together with details of how someone can commission you.
- A "links" page, where you add web links to things that interest you or that you want to promote, such as galleries you exhibit at, or craft guilds you belong to.
- A "news" page, which you update frequently with news of what you're up to.
- A blog – your blog can be integrated as part of your website.
- A gallery, showing images of your work. This can include animations to move from one image to the next; and you might want to organise it in sub-sections covering different types of work (for example, if you're a jeweller, you might separate your gallery into "rings" "brooches" "bracelets" etc.).

- Prices – even if you're not selling online, it's a good idea to give people an idea of your prices, so that if they turn up at a craft fair to buy a piece they have enough money!
- Recommendations – ask satisfied customers for comments and include hem on their own page or on your homepage.

When designing your site's navigation, it is important that wherever someone is, they can easily get to anywhere else on your site. This usually means having a navigation bar (at the top) or panel (on the left) on every page, with clickable links to every other page on your site.

A website should also integrate your social media presence. Usually this is in the form of clickable icons for Facebook, Twitter, Instagram, or whatever other networks you use, either on the homepage, or on every page. You can also provide Facebook "like" buttons on individual news items or blog posts.

Copyright

Copyright legislation is important. The text and images that you use on your site will be protected by copyright, but you should also ensure that you do not breach the copyright of others. If you publish copyright material on your website without permission, you risk legal action. Basic information on copyright is available from the Intellectual Property Office (IPO) website at www.ipo.gov.uk/c-basicfacts.pdf

You may be able to use another person's copyright material under license: go to www.ipo.gov.uk/copy/c-other/c-usebuy.htm for more information. If you engage someone else to design your website, make sure that you retain the copyright of the images and text on it.

Testing and maintaining your website

Once your website is built, you have to maintain it. Websites should be updated regularly with new content, or visitors will simply stop returning to your site, and rankings in search engines will be affected.

If you build your business website yourself, you can simply use the same tools you used initially to update your site's content. Photographs of new products, you exhibiting at a fair or an exhibition will all keep the site interesting to visitors.

If you hired a web designer to create your initial website, ask for a content management system so you can make changes to your site.

Once your site is up and running, you should visit it daily to ensure there are no technical problems preventing visitors from accessing it. You should regularly set aside time to check that all the links on the site work, and that graphics are not too large in file size (which will make them slow to download).

Remember to monitor visitor statistics by reviewing how many visitors go to the site, how long they stay there and which pages they go to. This can help you to identify whether your website is being used, and what changes may be required in the future. Your hosting company may provide a control panel that will give you access to basic stats; or you can use Google Analytics for free to get very comprehensive statistics (your web designer can help you set this up). Alternatively you can use a paid-for web-based service such as Alexa (www.alexa.com).

TOP TIP

Don't over-design your website. Some web designers are so consumed by the design that they create a site that is difficult to read.

CHAPTER 27

Selling online

Ecommerce

I f you've ever heard a group of makers or artists discussing ecommerce, you probably found that the verdict was evenly split on the topic of its worth. About half will think it's the best thing since sliced bread, while the other half find it too much of a hassle to coordinate the ordering, payment and shipping procedures. Deciding whether or not it suits you will depend on several factors.

Is your product suitable for ecommerce?

Virtually everything is available for purchase online. From miniatures to large sculptures, there seems to be a shipping option for just about any product. However it must be said that some products post more easily than others: jewellery travels well, whereas ceramics have to be packaged properly, which can add to the cost, and sending framed paintings to the USA can prove very expensive.

The law on selling online

You should be aware of the Consumer Protection (Distance Selling) Regulations 2000 and how these may affect your business. You can download a guide to the regulations from the Office of Fair Trading (OFT) website at www.oft.gov.uk/shared_oft/business_leaflets/general/oft698. pdf. More information on the Regulations can be found in BIF 333, A Guide to the Consumer Protection (Distance Selling) Regulations 2000.

There are a number of other pieces of legislation affecting selling via your website - these are explained in more detail in:

- BIF 342, An Introduction to Setting up an Online Store and
- BIF 351, An Introduction to Regulations Affecting E-commerce Businesses.

Under the Companies Act 2006, all electronic communications, websites and order forms (as well as all other hard and soft copy correspondence) must show the company's name, registered number, place of registration and registered office address.

Go to www.companieshouse.gov.uk/about/ pdf/gbf1.pdf and BIF 459, An Introduction to the Companies Act 2006 for further information.

Where to sell

As well as selling on your own website, there are numerous websites for craft workers and artists to market their goods. Some of the most popular ones are:

- Not on the High Street.com (NOTHS) – one of the most popular sites for creative work on the web. The demand for space on the site is huge and goods are carefully selected. It is expensive to join, but being on the site does give recognition to your brand.
- Etsy.com – an online venue for buying and selling handcrafted products. Like any online presence, maintaining an Etsy shop takes work. Etsy does, however, help people with marketing and suggestions to improve business. The site is widely used in the USA, so if you have customers there it could work well for you.

- Folksy.com – a site that sells handmade goods and craft supplies. It seems to have lower price points than NOTHS and is popular with traditional crafters.
- Artgallery.co.uk – a site that sells paintings on a commission basis. The site is well promoted, and artists seem to like the feedback from customers, which can be given over the site.
- Spreadshirt.co.uk – a site where designers can upload their designs and sell them printed onto t-shirts.

Saatchiart.com – the most prestigious online selling site is free to enter and only charges 30% commission. The only drawback is the number of artists from all over the world with whom you are competing.

Presenting your work properly

The photographs on your website must be as good as possible. People do not order from a website if the product image doesn't look good. Your customers can't touch your products on the Internet, so they are going to need an excellent image to give them that final push to click on the "Buy now" button. Your images must look perfect; good lighting makes all the difference, and if you are not good at digital photography then it's a good idea to go on a course.

If your site is for informational purposes only, you still need great images to attract customers to your craft shows and exhibitions. Good images can save you money too, since the website can replace a costly print catalogue.

Processing payments

The simplest option is to accept payments through a service such as PayPal. In this case you won't need any shopping cart software – PayPal does this for you, so you only need your PayPal account.

If you take credit card payments by phone, check with your merchant account provider to see which shopping cart software works with their system. You should also protect your customers by only using shopping cart software that uses a reliable cryptographic protocol to encrypt their personal data, such as SSL (secure sockets layer) or its successor, TLS (transport layer security).

It's important to give full details of your terms of trading on your site: this should include information on returns, methods of payment etc.

Shipping your customer orders

Before you start selling your products, you need to work out how you are going to send them to your customers. Always send a package to yourself first, to ensure that it arrives safely and to let you know how much it will cost. Investigate the various couriers and see which works best for you. Another shipping issue to consider is whether you are going to incorporate the cost of shipping into the cost of the product and offer "free" shipping, or whether the shipping will be an add-on to the cost of the sale.

TOP TIP

Include a thank-you card, personalised chocolate or small gift with the products; it makes people feel special and can help you increase repeat sales.

CHAPTER 28

Social Media

What is social media?

"Social media" refers to a type of website where people form online communities, and create and share content about things that interest them. It can be a cost-effective way to reach your customers and potential customers; it has a personal, interactive approach, which is ideal for craftworkers and artists, who often have a strong connection with their customers and enjoy communicating with them.

Popular social media sites include Facebook, Twitter, YouTube, LinkedIn, Pinterest, Flickr and Instagram, among others. They're all different, so have a look and establish which ones are most relevant for you. Once you join one, you become part of its community and can post information to it – news of a new product, links to information on your website, or simply opinions or news about the craft world. The key is that what you post must be interesting enough for a user to want to tell their friends about it.

How social media sites work

Social media sites vary, but they have certain basics in common:

- You join the community by signing up. Usually you provide your email address, and create a username (the name you'll be known by on the site) and a password.
- You create a profile – information about you or your business for others to see. You can choose how detailed to make it – you don't have to share everything!
- You build a network of other users who interest you. On Facebook, it's called "Friending" (for a person) and "Liking" (for a business), and on many other sites, it's called "Following"; it simply means that you connect with someone and receive the information they post. They might Like/Follow you back, which means they receive what you post.
- You post things to the site. You can post to all your contacts at once (on Facebook this is called a "status update", on Twitter, it's called a "Tweet"), or directly to one user. Your message can include photos, video, weblinks, etc. On some sites, you post in a specific medium, such as photos (Flickr, Instagram) or video (YouTube).
- Users respond to each other's content, e.g. by adding a comment, forwarding it to their contacts, or indicating that they find it interesting – on Facebook, this is called "Liking" a post, and on Twitter, you can "Favourite" a Tweet.

Being social

Social media is called "social" for a reason – it's all about two-way communication. People who only use it to "talk at" others, and to give out a marketing message, generally don't get very far – but those who interact, and share information on a range of topics, can end up with a big following. Some social media experts suggest the ratio of "posts about other things" to "posts promoting your business" should be as high as 9:1. This approach ensures you'll never be perceived as "spamming" people with your marketing, and is also more fun!

You needn't know someone personally to approach them on social media in a professional context. People are there to connect with others; so as long as your post is polite and relevant, it's fine. Just don't pester if you get no response.

Your online identity

Make your presence consistent on different social media sites, and try to echo your existing brand identity. So use your logo or photograph for a profile picture; customise your page with your business colours or a photo of your work; and choose a consistent username across different sites (ideally the same as your business name), to help people find you.

Facebook and Twitter are two of the most popular social media sites. Here's how they can help your business.

Facebook for business

Facebook has over a billion active users worldwide. It was once seen as "something for kids", but today that's far from true – the majority of users are aged 18 to 35. It was originally designed for individuals to keep in touch online; but as its popularity has grown, many businesses are recognising the advantages of having a Facebook presence.

Creating a profile

To use Facebook at all, you need to create a personal profile – go to www.facebook.com, click on "sign up". Remember, you can change your privacy settings to decide who can see what – some people make most of their profile private, so only their Facebook friends can see it.

Profile or Fan Page?

Some people use their personal profile as their business presence on Facebook. Technically, this is against Facebook's terms of service – but it's quite widely done.

But most people prefer to create a separate page (called a "Fan Page") for their business. A Fan Page gives you some extra functionality, such as analytics information (called "Insights") about who visits it. It also allows you to keep your personal life private. Another key difference is that a Page doesn't have "Friends" – it has "Fans". People don't have to send you a request to be a Fan, as they do before you become Friends – they just go ahead and click "Like".

At the top right of the screen is a drop-down menu where you can switch between postings as "you", or as your Fan Page – don't forget to set the appropriate one before you post!

Starting a group

Facebook groups are for users to share a common interest. Groups can be open (anyone can join) or private (people can't see content, or post any-thing, until you approve their request to join).

A Facebook group of your peers (e.g. craftworkers) can be a good way to network. A private group for your favoured customers could offer special content – vouchers or promotions – as a perk of membership. There are lots of other possibilities – look around at existing groups for ideas. Just ensure you have enough time to run the group well, and that it's worth the time you spend on it.

What to do on Facebook

Here are ten key things you can do to build a good Facebook network:

- Read the pages of people who interest you, and follow some of the links they post! You might find out interesting and useful things.
- "Like" the pages of people or organisations who interest you.
- Share other people's content on your own Page (click "share" at the end of their post). People appreciate this, and will be more likely to do the same for you.
- Comment on a post by someone else. Make your comment relevant, friendly, and not directly about your business, at least not the first time.
- Post something on someone's Page – perhaps a question about their work. Again, don't go straight in with promoting yourself.

- Create a poll on your Page (follow the "create poll" link) to conduct some market research with your Fans.
- Create an Event Page to promote an exhibition or event you're doing.
- When you connect with someone, see who else they Like – there might be people that you want to connect with too.
- Email your friends and contacts, asking them to Like your Page.
- Keep your Page regularly updated with plenty of rich content (photos, videos, news, comments, links to interesting sites), so that when people decide to check you out, they find lots to interest them.

Using apps on Facebook

Facebook apps (short for applications) are little add-ons to your profile or Page that help you do things. Many are silly and just for fun, but there's a whole section of business apps that can help you do things like collect email sign-ups, run offers and promotions, or integrate your blog with your Facebook page.

Advertising on Facebook

You can place small box adverts on Facebook. You create the ad on the site itself – a 25-character title, 135-character body text, an image, and a hyperlink. You can choose to target specific groups, based on the personal details they've provided in their profile (location, gender, age, etc.).

- You can pay either per click or per number or impressions. Per click is probably best, because people actually clicking on your ad is what matters.
- You can monitor results with the analysis tools Facebook provides. One-off deals are the best things to advertise, as people are more likely to pay attention to these than to general information about your business.

TOP TIP

Social media websites have very comprehensive Help pages. If you're unsure how to do something, search there for advice.

Twitter for business

Twitter allows people to interact online in short messages called Tweets. Tweets are limited to 140 characters (the length of a single text message on your phone), and can include links to photos, videos and websites.

There are over 200 million active Twitter accounts worldwide. Most of these have fewer than 50 Twitter contacts, mainly friends and celebrities. However, some analysts think that people are becoming increasingly keen to connect with brands and businesses as well. Twitter users tend to be better off than average, and they're very mobile – most access the site through a Smartphone or tablet.

Getting started

Ideally, your Twitter username should be the name of your business. But, as a Tweet is so short, you don't want anything longer than about 15 characters. Try to make any abbreviations meaningful. For example, if Linda Brown Ceramics becomes @LBC, that's nice and short, but it could mean anything! @LBCeramics might be a better choice. Something like @ ceramicsgirl could work, too, even though it doesn't match the business's name. It's great if you can then use the same name across other social media sites – it helps people find you, and helps you build a brand identity online.

Following and followers

Your Twitter experience is defined by who you follow, not by who follows you. So be selective! Start by following:

- your customers
- other craftworkers
- business contacts, e.g. suppliers, galleries, shops
- guilds and organisations you belong to
- funders, e.g. the Arts Council

On the left of your Twitter stream, you'll see "follow" suggestions from Twitter, based on who you already follow. Twitter can also scan your email address book to help you find people you know. You can look at the Twitter accounts of people who are influential in your network, and see who they follow; and you can search Twitter using keywords such as "crafts" to find people involved in your field.

It's best to add people reasonably slowly – no more than 20 or 30 a day – rather than hundreds at once, which could get you banned for aggressive following. And when you get a new follower, remember you don't have to follow back unless you want to.

What to Tweet

As with any social network, the ratio of "content about other things" to "content promoting your work" should be quite high. Look at what other people Tweet about to get some ideas. It's good to include rich content, like a photo or weblink; and it's great to respond to others and engage in conversation.

- Tell people about your work, describe new work, post a link to video blogs.
- Share information by telling people about craft fairs and opportunities. Analyse your audience by using Search twitter.com to find out what people are thinking about crafts.
- Announce new developments – are you opening a shop on Etsy? Taking part in a craft fair? Build relationships with your followers by telling them.
- Keep people in touch: let them know if your website is down for any reason, and update when it is repaired.
- You can use Twitter to take commissions, custom requests, or orders via Tweets or direct messages. Keep customers up to date on the progress of their order.

Hashtags

A "hashtag" means placing the hash symbol (#) in front of an important keyword in your Tweet. Readers can then click on the hashtag to see all other Tweets containing the same tag, linking your Tweet to what others are saying. However, don't overdo it – it can be #annoying if #someone makes a #hashtag out of #every #other #word! track who's clicked on your links.

TOP TIP

Although Tweeting is usually immediate, never Tweet when you're angry or upset – you can easily say something you'll regret.

Using Twitter to drive traffic to your website

Create a Tweet around a link to something on your website, with a compelling headline-style message to encourage people to click on it, such as "Sting buys wife #ceramic brooch at #craft fair, see my other designs @..."

Twitter will automatically shorten any weblink you include – but an even better way is to use a URL-shortener such as bitly.com or ow.ly, which let you track who's clicked on your links.

Instagram for business

Instagram is a social networking phone app, which can only be used from an Apple iPhone. It is becoming very popular amongst creative people. It allows you to take photos and post them online, using the built-in filters to add text or to make the photo look better. Your followers can then share, like and comment on your photos. The best way to start is by becoming a regular user, watching what others do, and considering how this will fit into your marketing. Here are some tips for using Instagram effectively:

- As with any other social network, don't keep posting constant photographs of your product, or your followers will get fed up. You can get your followers engaged with your product without being too "promotional" – for example, introduce new staff or members of your family, show your products in situ so people can see how they will work in their own homes, show people wearing or using your products in interesting situations. 20% of your content should be about your products, and 80% should be about other things.

- Co-ordinate Instagram with your other social media, and if possible use the same name as your Twitter account, so that when your content is tagged and shared on Twitter the @username links to your Twitter bio.
- Remember your customer profile, and watch what your potential customers are posting. Create sneak previews – everyone loves to know a secret, so show your followers what you are making before you launch it.
- If you want to make a big impression, remember that images involving cute animals and funny quotations are the most likely to go viral.
- Using the filters effectively does make a massive difference to your audience, and can turn an average photo into something spectacular. For example, the retro filters can give a sense of vintage style that people will like: remember the famous Hovis advertisement!
- Don't jump around; keep some consistency, follow a theme and show your brand's personality.
- Calls to action work well – place the call to action on the image to grab people's attention.
- Read your feedback and learn from it.

Other social media

New social media sites are springing up all the time. If you find ones that work for you, stick with them, but don't neglect trying new ones. If one isn't working for you, then close your account down rather than just leaving it un-updated, which can look bad. Keeping up to date with social media can be very time-consuming, so don't waste your time on sites which are no longer working for you.

CHAPTER 29

Blogging

Some craftworkers and artists base their online presence around a blog. A blog is basically an online diary, which gives readers regular updates on you and your business. With so many creative people blogging, it can be difficult to make your blog stand out; but here are some tips to help you attract readers and make your mark.

Getting started

Your first decision is choosing a blogging platform. There are lots of free options available, including Wordpress, Tumblr, TypePad and Blogger. They all offer free design themes to let you customise how your blog looks. If you need help on how things work, the platform you choose will have its own Help pages, or you can find video tutorials on YouTube and elsewhere.

Linking up

Always link your blog to the rest of your online presence. If you don't have a website yet, you can start a blog anyway, and add links to your main website when you set one up. Market your blog just as you would your website: include links to it on your business cards, email signature, Twitter bio and Facebook page. In your blog posts, include in-text links to relevant areas of your website, your YouTube or Flickr pages, etc; and include social sharing buttons at the end of your blog posts.

What should you blog about?

Your blog should be about a specific topic. This way, your readers will know what to expect, and search engines will find your content more easily. It can work well to pick a subject that is indirectly related to your business – for example, if you make art with recycled materials, you could blog about all aspects of recycling. Give information that your readers will value and find useful – tips, ideas, news, how-to's, and so on. If you're stuck for a topic, try reading other blogs aimed at a similar audience. The subjects covered might give you ideas; and the comments from readers will show you what your community cares about and what gets them talking.

Ask readers to contribute

Turn your blog into a discussion. Ask people to add comments or questions; invite feedback; respond to people's contributions; build a community and be friendly. Make commenting easy, and write about things that get people talking. If people can interact on your blog, they'll keep coming back.

Don't be afraid of criticism

Negative comments can be upsetting, particularly if they are critical of your work. But if you do get a negative comment on your blog, don't worry. Any comments you're really not happy with can always be deleted; but it's better to respond to them positively if you can. People's feedback, even the negative things, can be really useful if you're prepared to learn from it – but this doesn't mean you need to take every comment to heart. And it's very rare that you'll face serious negativity, so don't worry about it too much.

Use images

The internet is very visual, and good photographs are important. You are promoting your own products, so there should always be images of them, but don't forget pictures of your stall at a craft fair, photographs of you at work, and so on. Images are essential to a good creative blog, so provide as many as possible and give your audience lots to enjoy.

Be easy to read

Research suggests that people skim-read the text on a website, rather than reading every last word. So try to make your articles easy, quick reads. Bullet points and short paragraphs make it easier to read. Don't let your posts get too long, either. You need around 300 words per post to enable a search engine to pick it up; but don't go much longer than this.

Use eye-catching titles

When thinking about things to blog about, write articles that have punchy titles: ones that are appealing and catchy, and that include phrases that people might search for through search engines.

Blog regularly

A blog needs to be kept up regularly. Try to post at least two articles a week. If you make use of scheduling tools on your blog, you can write several articles in advance, and post them automatically while you're away from your desk. You can even blog from your phone. If you have the technology, blogging from a craft fair can be interesting for your followers.

Be yourself

Write the way you speak, and let your personality come through. Be conversational, not formal, and avoid jargon. On the other hand, don't go too informal – readers don't enjoy posts that are full of chatroom slang. Try reading a post out loud before you publish it, to see if it reads well and sounds natural.

Get personal

Although it might surprise you, people will be interested in you and what you are doing. So tell people about yourself, and your family and friends – but don't forget that your primary purpose is to build your business. Photographs of you wearing your jewellery, or you with a celebrity (even if it's only the local Mayor!) will add personal interest whilst keeping the focus on your business.

Proof-read your posts

Always check what you have written before you post it - it's easy to make mistakes. Bad spelling will not only ruin your credibility, it will damage your search-engine rankings, as search engines can't pick up a misspelled word. So check over your spelling and grammar thoroughly.

TOP TIPS

Include a call to action in a blog post e.g. invite readers to comment, or join you on Twitter, or visit you at a craft fair or exhibition.

Give something away: run an online competition for a prize, or offer freebies or discounts to your readers.

CHAPTER 30
Other ways to use the Internet

Video

Any visual imagery is good for a creative business. People love watching videos, so a video can improve your website's traffic. Making a video is easy, but making a professional-looking video needs thought and planning. If you are being videoed making your product or teaching a skill, practice until you are perfect. Sometimes it helps to be interviewed, so find a friend to ask you questions.

You should have a clear idea of why you're making a video: is it to increase traffic to your website? Are you trying to get work teaching? You can pack a lot of information into a simple 3-minute video, but remember not to give all your secrets away!

You can just put a video straight onto your own website. But it can be better to put it on Youtube instead – YouTube is a social media community, which might mean that your video will get seen more widely. It also means you're not using up your own website's bandwidth to host the video. YouTube provides you with a link you can use to embed the video on your own site, if you want to display it there as well.

Sometimes videos catch the public imagination and get huge numbers of hits. This is rarely planned; the public are fickle and the strangest things become hits. Remember that videos have a worldwide audience, so keep the dialogue simple.

Crowdfunding

Crowdfunding is a way of raising money for a specific project or business. You create a profile of your project and post it on a crowdfunding website, stating how much you want to raise. Profiles are free, but the site will generally charge between 3% and 12.5% for processing donations. You then offer rewards to donors at different levels; e.g. donate £50 and get a DVD of the project, or donate £200 and be invited to the premiere.

Crowdfunding can work well for certain creative projects, but remember that over 50% of the projects on Kickstarter (a popular crowdfunding site) fail. Film projects have one of the best success rates. To be successful, you need to capture the public imagination, and have a strong social media presence.

If you are interested in using this as a source of start-up capital, there are some good articles about it online, and workshops are available through Eventbrite.

Eventbrite

Eventbrite is a site on which you can promote your workshops, exhibitions and other events. It allows you to manage, promote and sell your tickets using simple online tools. It's a useful way of promoting workshops, although it seems to be more active in urban areas. See www.eventbrite.co.uk for details.

Newsletters

Newsletters can be a very effective means of promotion, providing a link between craftworker and customer. They can be used to advertise your presence at shows, to launch new products, or to remind customers of your range. You can use desktop publishing software to design your newsletter, or there are several online tools that help you do it. As well as distributing by email, you might want to print some copies to give to customers at craft fairs, or include with orders. If you don't want the task of regular blogging, sending out a newsletter four times a year might be a better option.

Do include personal information if you enjoy having a social relationship with your customers. Many of them become friends over the years, and like to keep in touch. Some of the best newsletters involve the customers in the business by sharing details that they wouldn't have otherwise known.

Use illustrations where possible. Add a photograph, scan in a drawing, or use copyright-free clip art.

Newsletters are most effective if produced on a regular basis. Every three months is a good interval, unless you have something special to announce sooner. You can include special offers, discount vouchers, or even carry advertising for fellow craftworkers to help with the cost. Details of interesting commissions, exhibitions, prizes won or the use of new materials are all of interest to your customers. If you find it difficult to think of something to write, think of the type of questions you are asked at craft fairs; this is the type of information that is most likely to appeal to your readers.

MailChimp

If you intend to send out regular email newsletters and updates to a large mailing list, then signing up to a site like MailChimp can save you a lot of time. For it to be effective you need a strong email list. You can design your own emails using MailChimp's templates, gather information on your list, and produce a more professional mailing easily.

Part 6

Resources

Resources

Web addresses of organisations are given throughout the book for your information. We repeat some of them here, with telephone numbers and postal addresses for those who do not have access to the Internet.

Art and craft organisations
The Crafts Council

44a, Pentonville Road, Islington,
London N1 9BY
Tel. 020 7806 2500
www.craftscouncil.org.uk

The Crafts Council is the national body for promoting contemporary crafts. It runs the National Centre for Craft and Design, which houses the Gallery and Gallery Shop, the Reference Library and Picture Library, and has a photostore containing the work of craftworkers.

Arts Council England

14 Great Peter Street London SW1P 3NQ
Tel 0845 300 6200
www.artscouncil.org.uk

Arts Council England supports creative and artistic projects throughout the UK. They have a number of regional offices and offer funding and advice.

The Prince's Trust

Prince's Trust House
9 Eldon Street
London EC2M 7LS
Tel: 020 7543 1234
www. princes-trust.org.uk

The Prince's Trust offers advice, help and support for people aged between 18-30 who want to start their own business.

Prime

Tavis House, London WC1H 9NA Tel: 020 3137 8525 www.prime.org.uk
Prime is a charity that helps people over 50 to set up their own businesses.

a-n

The Toffee Factory,
Lower Steenbergs Yard Quayside
Newcastle upon Tyne NE1 6AB Tel: 0300 330 0706 www.a-n.co.uk

a-n is an organisation for visual artists. Membership includes insurance and other benefits.

Society for All Artists (SAA)

PO Box 50
Newark
Nottinghamshire NG23 5GY
Tel: 0845 300 7753
www.saa.co.uk

The SAA is an organization for everyone who loves painting, memberships includes insurance. They also offer an online shop

British Jewellers' Association (BJA)
Federation House
10 Vyse Street Birmingham B18 6LT
Tel 0121 237 1110
www.bja.org.uk

The BJA is the national trade association for the British jewellery and silversmithing industry.

Association of Woodturners
Windrush,
High Street,
Drybrook,
Glos. GL17 9ET
www.woodturners.co.uk

A non-profit organisation for the advancement and promotion of woodturning.

TextileArtist
www.textileartist.org

An online resource and community for artists working with textiles.

The Greeting Card Association
United House
North Road
London N7 9DP
Tel 020 7619 0396
www.greetingcardassociation.org.uk

This is the trade association for the greeting card industry. Their website contains useful information for freelance designers.

Small business organisations
Federation of Small Businesses

Sir Frank Whittle Way,
Blackpool
Lancashire FY4 2FE
Tel: 0808 20 20 888
www.fsb.org.uk

The Forum of Private Business

Ruskin Chambers,
Drury Lane,
Knutsford,
Cheshire WA16 6HA
Tel: 0845 130 1722
www.fpb.org

National Market Traders' Federation

Hampton House
Hawshaw Lane
Hoyland
Barnsley S74 0HA
Tel: 01226 749 021
www.nm□.co.uk

The NMTF offers services to their members including insurance, chip and pin and information on fairs and market. Some markets, including farmers' markets, insist on membership of this organisation in order to rent a stall.

Copyright and data protection
ACID- Anti Copying in Design

68 Lombard Street
London EC3V 9LJ
Tel 0845 6443617
www.acid.uk.com

CopyWatch

CopyWatch is the compliance arm of the Copyright Licensing Agency Ltd. It offers design protection for members of the Giftware Association; this is accessed through the Giftware Association's website,

www.ga- uk.org

Information Commissioner's Office

Wycliffe House
Water Lane
Wilmslow
Cheshire
SK9 5AF
Tel: 0303 123 1113
www.ico.org.uk

The ICO is the UK's independent authority on data protection and freedom of information.

Publications

Subscribing to a regular publication can be a vital lifeline, providing up- to-date information on your craft, the general market, and opportunities. There are many publications, which may be appropriate for you. If you don't know where to start, check out the following:

Craft & Design

P.O. Box 5
Driffield
East Yorkshire YO25 8JD
Tel: 01377 255 213 www.craftanddesign.net

Crafts

Crafts is the magazine for the Crafts Council. Access through their website
www.craftscouncil.org.uk

Ceramic Review

63 Great Russell Street London WC1B 3BF
Tel 020 7183 5583 www.ceramicreview.com
The magazine for contemporary ceramic art and craft.

Index

www.ingramcontent.com/pod-product-compliance
Lightning Source LLC
Chambersburg PA
CBHW052001090426
42741CB00008B/1502